“One Voice”

"One Voice"

Speak Out, America—Raise Your Voice—
It Matters!

Ervin Hendrix, Jr.

Order this book online at www.trafford.com
or email orders@trafford.com

Most Trafford titles are also available at major online book retailers.

Printed in the United States of America.

ISBN: 978-1-4269-0031-0(sc)

Our mission is to efficiently provide the world's finest, most comprehensive book publishing service, enabling every author to experience success. To find out how to publish your book, your way, and have it available worldwide, visit us online at www.trafford.com

Trafford rev. 10/21/2010

Trafford PUBLISHING www.trafford.com

North America & international
toll-free: 1 888 232 4444 (USA & Canada)
phone: 250 383 6864 • fax: 812 355 4082

To the joys of my life—my devoted wife, children, grandchildren, and great-granddaughter

Contents

Introduction

Hurricane Katrina, possibly one of the worst natural disasters to occur in the history of the United States, was the instrument that inspired me to write this book. This disaster illustrated, in my opinion, many of the critical shortcomings of our governments and many of our citizens, including myself. As I write this book, it is not to criticize any individual or attempt to place blame. It is a simple man sharing a few of his life experiences in the hope that sharing these experiences and opinions will encourage and motivate others of similar experiences to do likewise and to help bring about changes in our nation.

This disaster really bothered me. Maybe the reason it affected me the way it did is because my wife and I had visited New Orleans for the first time two weeks before the hurricane. One of the workers at the hotel we stayed in befriended my wife. The day we departed, the worker did not come to work because she was a single parent with two daughters and had to get materials for them to go back to school. She worked at the hotel six days a week.

As the television camera's scanned the masses on the grounds of the convention center and super dome. The images disturbed me enormously, as I sat watching the major news networks with their different anchor people and commentators commenting on the enormity of the disaster in New Orleans. There was much speculation as to who was responsible for the lack of immediate action in responding to this catastrophic disaster. People asked many questions. Was it because of race or class? As I sat watching the news, I could not help but think of the gentle woman who had befriended my wife and wonder about her situation. I prayed that she and her children survived the disaster.

This disaster caused me to ask myself many questions, including those questions asked by the news media. After much thought, I concluded that both elements were involved—race and class. The irony is that many of us were and are still displaying behavior similar to behavior displayed by those living in caste system societies. Sadly, far too many of us are involved in behavior that created those conditions in New Orleans.

In many of our larger cities, certain segments of our society are living under conditions similar to those that existed in New Orleans prior to Hurricane Katrina. Millions of outstanding citizens have worked and are working diligently today to improve the conditions that existed and still exist in New Orleans. They require much additional help.

That hurricane caused me to search deep within myself, and much of what I discovered causes me pain and sadness. In my efforts to be a good law-abiding citizen, rising from generations of traceable poor Georgia sharecroppers, I have failed the most important duty of being a good citizen. This failure was not intentional. It was mere ignorance on my part of how important individual participation is in our governmental systems.

This disaster has caused me to find my voice. It is but one voice, but never again will this voice be silent on issues that I feel adversely affect me or my country, state, city, community, and family. The majority of the victims of this disaster were poor. Many lived below the poverty level in a country of plenty. I asked myself, what is the function of government? Is it the responsibility of government to establish laws in the best interest of all citizens? Is it to provide protection for its citizens? What is the government's role?

After careful analysis, my answer is that the government's function is whatever we, the citizens, want it to be. However, you and I must be engaged in every facet at every level. Hurricane Katrina was a natural disaster of catastrophic proportions. However, officials predicted years in advance that a hurricane of Katrina's magnitude would devastate New Orleans.

Many are asking how the government could have failed to reinforce and strengthen those levies around New Orleans with all the data that was available.

Many of the citizens of New Orleans must share in the responsibility for the lack of immediate positive response to the disaster. Over the years, they did not speak out demanding that those levies be reinforced, nor did they demand that their political leaders take positive action regarding many of their community concerns. It was not because they did not care, like many Americans, including myself, they were too busy focusing on everyday living, trying to secure a better future for their children and grandchildren. They elected their government officials, placed their trust and confidence in them, to do what was best for them. The members of the middle-class, was struggling to maintain their status, and the poor were expending all of their energy trying to survive.

Our elected officials are good people. I feel that the majority of them are sincere in their efforts and that they believe they are performing the service their constituents want. The problem is that they are hearing mostly from the elite and wealthier populations of their communities—the minority—those who have the time to visit them or who can afford to hire lobbyists to lobby on their behalf. People who are members of private country clubs and can afford to invite these elected officials to those country clubs for the purpose of influencing their decisions on matters of public interest. These elite populations are good people and citizens of our nation. However, a majority of them cannot relate to the conditions of our daily lives.

We, the middle class and poor populations, must advocate our concerns to our elected officials by written communication, verbal communication, and at the ballot box. We must demand that our elected officials represent our interests, not only those of special interest groups. I implore all to join me, express your ideas and opinions to your elected representatives, and let's hold them accountable to us. Should they fail to listen or respond, let's use our ballot on Election Day to deliver the message we intend to be heard.

When I first gave serious thought to writing this book, I asked myself what had I to say that was important enough for one to devote his or her time reading it. I decided to share a few of my life experiences in the hopes that doing so would provide reasoning as to why Americans must become more involved. There is nothing unusual or exceptional about my life or experiences. Millions of men in America live and have lived similar lives.

After giving much consideration to the idea, I decided that the main reason for sharing my story and experiences is that it is men like me, whose stories are untold, that contribute toward many of these conditions. Perhaps, if more of us share our stories and experiences, we will be able to create changes within the mind of many of our fellow citizens. A change in thoughts and behavior on behalf of many Americans is needed to eliminate many of society's problems—such as those that existed and still exist in New Orleans.

This book is a personal plea to people of all ethnic backgrounds and social statuses to help change these deplorable conditions existing in our country. As I express opinions, I'll be expressing those that are based on the black experience as I have experienced it in our country. If anything said or implied is offensive to anyone, I sincerely apologize. I'm extending a personal plea to you, the readers of this book. You deserve to know how I think and why I think the way, I do. Like many of our citizens, I consider myself a good citizen of this country, a man who believes in faith, trust, and support of our system of government.

Like many of you, I have served my country in combat and retired honorably from the United States Army. I have voted in every election since becoming of age. I have been a Scoutmaster of a Boy Scout troop, and I have coached and managed youth baseball and softball teams. I have mentored and tutored young men and women and have voluntarily taught at a school for youth at risk. I have been a member and leader of several social organizations.

Like many, my spouse and I have worked hard to provide for our family, educate our children, buy our house, and try to live the American dream. We have been blessed with good health and much luck. We have reached a point in life whereby one would classify our status as middle class. There is nothing unusual about my life. I worked hard and overcame many obstacles, the same as majority of Americans.

However, there is one aspect of my life that was very troublesome for me. This part of my life caused me tremendous hurt, heartache, and deeply affected my personality. This aspect of my life gave me the experience, knowledge, and in-depth insight into what I feel to be one of our nation's greatest problems. I feel that it's important to share my experiences in the hopes that my experiences will illuminate the plight of many of our children. Although I can only speak from one individual's black American experiences,

I wish to share them with the hope that they give cause for us to reflect on our most precious resources—our children. Therefore, I'll start with a few of my life experiences from the beginning as I recall them.

My Early Remembrances

Life for me began on January 13, 1941, in Screven County, Georgia, on a farm in a rural area. I'm the oldest of thirteen children born to my parents. My first remembrance of a house is of an old wooden building sitting on wooden supports elevated off the ground. I remember this clearly. I had crawled under the house playing and was trying to catch this thing, which I later learned was a snake, crawling along the rafters. My mother came looking for me just as I was reaching for the snake. She screamed; her yell was terrifying. I also remember the wood-burning stove and the fireplace. The stove was used to cook meals. In the winter months, it was used along with the fireplace in an attempt to keep the house warm. I also remember everyone sitting close to the fireplace to keep warm in the winter months.

My next memory about my birthplace is of a red dirt road. At the time, I didn't know what dirt or red was. All I knew was that when it rained and my parents took me to visit my grandmothers' home our feet would get wet and dirty. It was about this time in my life when my parents thought I should learn to pray. The first prayer they taught me was a child's prayer. It was something like:

> Now I lay down to sleep, I pray the Lord my soul to keep. If I die before I wake, I pray the Lord my soul to take.

This was a simple prayer to learn, but what followed began a series of sad and heartbreaking events in my life. I share these events with you because there is a particular segment of our country's children who I'm deeply hurt and saddened for. My hope is to encourage at least one person to help change one of these young lives for the better. Although I have other early memories, none is as vivid as the ones I will be sharing with you. These memories had a lasting impact on my life. So what? Life goes on and we must adjust.

This was the beginning of what I considered in my early years to be an abusive and cruel childhood. It began before I started school. I think I was around four or five years old. As I said earlier, my parents decided that it was time for me to learn to pray. After learning the first prayer, they decided it was time I learned the Lord's Prayer. I had no trouble learning it verbatim up to the verse, "But deliver us from evil," for some reason, I had a problem remembering that verse.

My father thought the way to teach me was to whip me. Notice I didn't say *spank me*; I said *whip me*. This had the opposite effect of his desire. Instead of me concentrating on learning the phrase, I concentrated on the whipping I knew was coming. Of course, it took me twice as long to learn the prayer. It was also about this time that I began to think that my only worth to my father was the little work he could get out of me.

One night, my father remembered something he had left at the edge of the field behind our house that he needed. It was one of those very dark nights, or it appeared so to me. He told me to go and get the item. Of course, I was scared, as any four- or five-year-old child would be. However, I went and got it. That incident started many unsupervised trips to my grandmother's house at night. She probably lived about a half mile from my parents' house. But can you imagine a four- or five-year-old walking that distant alone after dark?

Of course, there was no traffic for my parents to worry about running me over. In fact, there was no one walking the road except me. There was no light other than moonlight if the moon was out. Much of the distance was covered by forest, and the only sounds I would hear were the sounds of animals.

This was frightening, and at that age, I remember thinking that something was wrong with having to walk that dark road by myself. As I have often thought back to those days, it *was* wrong. However, what is much worse today is that too many children are living under conditions much worse than my conditions were. They are not living on sharecropper farms. They are living in the ghetto farms of our large cities. As I recall my youth and the conditions I was raised under, I'm grateful my father was there to beat me. He was there to send me up those dark roads. He was also working hard in those fields to feed me, clothe me, and see that I had a house to sleep in at night, with both parents present, even though there were holes in the walls throughout the house.

After becoming an adult and reflecting back on that period, I understand why I was sent to my grandmother's house alone on those nights. My father was completely exhausted from working those fields from sunup to sunset. Fathers, whatever culture you are a member of, can your children say that they are eating and sleeping securely tonight because you are there sharing in their heartache and pains, doing the best you can, whatever it is? As I share segments of my life story, I'll be speaking from the experiences I know as a black man growing up in America.

These experiences are shared for the benefit of all fathers and sons—fathers who are without employment, fathers confined in penal institutions, fathers who have abandoned their children and their children's moms, fathers who have given up on society and the world we live in, and particularly those fathers who have benefitted from the wealth of our nation.

When I say "wealth of our nation," I mean items of true value, such as equal opportunity for a good education, equal justice under our judicial system, and equal opportunity for employment. I ask that we examine and reexamine ourselves closely. Have we done what we can to change the situation, rather than find external reasons for our conditions?

Even in my father's cruelest hour toward me—and there were many cruel hours—reflecting back as an adult, I realize that he did his best as he knew to raise me. As fathers, we owe our children our best. Our best may not be as good as our neighbors', but if it's our best, our children will recognize it as they grow and mature.

There are many fathers that don't have their children's mothers in their lives. Hostility may exist between many of us and our children's mothers. This should have no effect on our doing the best we can to help her support our child. This child is a part of us.

My next memory is of the period when I first entered formal school. It was a one-room shack about a mile from the house my parents were living in. I recall my parents having moved twice between the house with the snake under it and the one we were living in when I started school. The school was a wooden building with cracks and holes throughout. In the winter months, the teacher and children would huddle around the wood-burning stove, attempting to keep warm. My first teacher was an elderly woman who was devoted to children. She was my mother's first teacher. Her name was Ida Barnes. Mrs. Barnes taught more than one grade in that little wooden building. The school's name was Ditch Pond. I went to Ditch Pond for about four years. My parents moved to two other farms while I attended Ditch Pond. I changed schools several times before entering high school.

The years between the ages of five and thirteen were hectic and difficult years for me. Every year, my family moved. Making friends was difficult to do. As I grew older, my father's behavior became more abusive toward me. Over the years, as I have reflected back trying to analyze and closely evaluate my father's behavior when dealing with me, I've gained a much better understanding and appreciation of him, the overall man.

He did many things that I know were wrong, but they were done out of ignorance. In many ways, he was a good man. He was the second-to-last child of a farmer and preacher. His parents had sixteen children. He had a sixth-grade education. I mention this because I'm going to be talking about my father throughout this book as I address fathers and young men. My father's actions deeply affected who I am today, perhaps more than any person I know—the bad as well as the good things he did.

Why is this important? Because fathers, if I can get you to relate to any of the issues I grew up facing and understand how they affected me, maybe you will find something in what I'm saying to help you in dealing with your children. I also hope that you young men who read this book will find something that will help you to cope with the adversities in your life—something to motivate you to be good fathers and productive members of society.

As said earlier, I'm the oldest of thirteen children. Therefore, at an early age, my father had me in the fields helping him farm. On many days, I would get home from school and head straight for the fields. Often I would return home just before darkness and then gather wood for cooking and heating the house. We had no electricity; we lit the house with kerosene lanterns. What studying I did for school was by lantern light or light emanating from the fire in the fireplace. This was bad on the eyes.

My father grew up in rural Georgia in the 1920s. An education for the vast majority of black children during that period meant learning how to write their names. The work on the farms was hard, and the children were expected to help their parents tend the crops. They were called sharecroppers. This meant that blacks would work the crops produced on the farms and share in the profits.

Of course, whites also worked those farms. However, their conditions were not as deplorable. These sharecroppers made very little money and had to buy many of the items they needed on credit from the general store. The owner of the farms they were working often owned these stores. At the end of the year when the crops were harvested, my parents—like many others—would still be indebted to the landowner. The landowner was the bookkeeper, and his word was the law. If he was dishonest, the sharecropper was more or less his slave to work his farm. I have lasting memories of the period from the late 1940s through the early 1960s. Life was not very good for blacks in rural Georgia.

Early Life in Rural Georgia

On several occasions in the late 1940s and early 1950s, I would hear white men call to my father, "Hey, boy, do this or do that." I remember that some of my father's first advice to me was to never question the white man, to always say, "Yes, sir," and to never look at or say anything to a white woman. To a small child, the significance of this message was not clear. I remember that he would carry me to the small town closest to where we lived. We would enter the establishments through the rear door into a room with a large hole cut into the wall for blacks to order through. I remember the signs on those establishments that said White Only and Colored.

Going into that little town with my parents was exciting for me. My father would carry me to the barbershop to get a haircut every time he went. The barber was a friendly, elderly man. His customers would come in, and they and my father would laugh and talk. My father was always good to me on those occasions, as were all the men in the barbershop. My dad was a good baseball player, and he and many of the other black sharecroppers would play baseball on Saturday afternoons for entertainment. They would have their whole families out cheering for their teams.

My father spent much time throwing a baseball with me and carrying me to the baseball field to play baseball with other fathers and sons. He would often take me fishing in the late afternoons and early evenings after the farm work was complete. He taught me how to hunt at an early age. I was around ten or eleven years old when he bought me my first gun. It was a .22-caliber rifle. We would spend much of his spare time hunting. When he couldn't hunt during the daylight hours, he would carry me at nights with him. Shortly after giving me a rifle, he brought me a .410-gauge shotgun and taught me how to shoot it and hunt wild rabbits.

After I became an adult and had somewhat experienced life, I began to realize that my father was showing me love in the only way he knew. I cannot to this day ever remember my father saying, "I love you." Yet as I grew and matured, I realized that he had a great love for me and expressed it in many ways and in words that were hard for a young mind to comprehend. It's very easy for the mind of young people to be shaped by negative things communicated to them, especially when communicated by their parents. I often think back to those days when I swore I would kill my father on my sixteenth birthday. I am grateful to whatever reason or thing that changed my mind, because over the years, I've come to understand many things my young mind could not comprehend or appreciate during that period.

Why did I ever think I wanted to kill my father? On many occasions, if I did not perform to the standards my father desired, he became angry and said things much worse to me than any beating. Two of his favorite sayings were "You are not worth the gunpowder it would take to kill you with" and "You are not worth the salt in the bread you eat." These two statements had a devastating effect on me. He started saying them to me when I was about eight years old and would say one of them every time he was displeased with me about something.

Another of his sayings was "You'll be in jail before you are sixteen years old." Again, he began saying this before I was ten years old. I developed such a dislike for him and those utterances that at some point around the age of ten, I made up my mind that he was correct. I *would* be in jail by the time I reached the age of sixteen, and it would be for killing him. It was during these years that I would spend all of my hours when not in school working the farm. In the spring, I often plowed the fields, working with a mule. After plowing the fields, we would plant cotton, corn, peanuts, and so on. Once the crops were growing, we cultivated them by hoeing and plowing them to keep the weeds from growing.

During the summer and fall months, we picked cotton and harvested the crops before winter. I remember this being hard, backbreaking work. We often left home before the sun came up and returned well after dark. The older I became, the worse my father's demeanor became toward me. I remember crying many times, wondering what it was that caused him to feel the way he did toward me.

During this period, I was a young child, and school meant very little if anything to me. Most of the children I knew or played with were at school. We had no close neighbors, and those who lived on the neighboring farms were as busy working the farms as I was. This might seem irrelevant to most people, but as I have often reflected back over my life, I cannot remember having hope or dreams beyond those farms. As I look back to my children and grandchildren's lives, I realize that one of the major ingredients of a young life is the ability to dream and hope. It's natural for a child to dream and to pretend. It's those dreams and the pretending that provides hope. My dream or goal as a youngster growing up was to kill my father. Fathers, I cannot overemphasize the hurt and damage done to a child abused and mistreated in his or her formative years.

Men, it's critical that children have a positive influence and role model in their lives. Middle-class fathers, there can be no better example in a child's life than us. We have found success in our lives and represent the perfect mentor for our young people. I'll address several ways we can do this later.

We moved to the city of Savannah when I was thirteen. I found little odd jobs, cutting grass in people's yards and delivering newspapers. My father took what little money I made. His behavior toward me became worse, much more verbal than physically abusive. I would rush home from school and try to find work or anything to avoid being around him. When I could not avoid being away from home, I read any book available to keep from being around him.

It was still my intention to kill him for my sixteenth birthday; I told my mother this many times. Her replies would always be the same. "Son, pray and ask God to guide you. Please don't think that way." Once children feel useless and worthless, life stops having meaning for them. When one is told that he or she is not worth the gunpowder it would take to kill him or her with or the salt in the bread he or she eats, it destroys all hope within that child—or at least it did for me. I found this hard to understand, much less put my faith in God.

Again, my father was there. I had food to eat, a place to sleep, and I was going to school. Can you imagine what the homeless child must feel like? I felt hopeless and useless growing up under the conditions I grew up under. In my early years, there was no television to broadcast the more pleasant aspects of life. Today, our young people see the surrounding world through the view of the media. This media creates an avenue of hope and dreams for them.

Can you imagine the child who is hungry, homeless, and motherless or fatherless seeing the possibilities life offers through the media? Can you imagine how those children, who are not able to eat a nourishing meal, take a good hot shower, put on clean clothes, and feel safe sleeping at night feel?

Fathers, there are far too many of our children living under these conditions. I don't believe we can call ourselves good citizens of our communities without addressing the conditions that contribute to too many of the factors that affect these children.

Sometime around the age of fifteen, maybe from reading one of those books I would read to occupy my mind and take it off the abuse I was subjected to, the thought came into my mind. *You don't want to kill your father for your sixteenth birthday; he is not worth you going to jail.* The abuse didn't stop, but I began to adapt or adjust and became more emboldened by the thought that killing him was not worth going to jail.

Meeting of a Mentor

It was at about this time in my life that I met a young man who had returned from the Korean War. He would sit and talk with a group of us young fellows, telling us to stay in school at least until we were of age to join the army, and then we could join the army if we couldn't do anything else. He encouraged us to avoid doing anything that would lead toward jail. My mother was also a strong advocate of my finishing high school. I made up my mind that I was going to finish high school.

To this day, I don't know that young man's given name. I know his family name and his nickname. I often think of him and of how much his talks and advice meant to me. I don't know how many other young men's lives he affected, but I do know what a positive influence he was in my life. The sad thing is that he will never know how much of an influence he had on my life because I never said thank you to him. In fact, it was many years later when I realized just how much of an impact he'd made on me. I'm grateful today that he came into my life. Because of this man, I have dedicated many hours trying to encourage and motivate young children to dream, hope, and, most of all, stay in school and get good grades. I have stressed the importance of education.

Throughout high school, I worked. In the eleventh and twelfth grades, I worked in country-and-western nightclubs as a waiter until 2:00 AM, five nights a week. An incident happened one night at one of the clubs. The police came to the door and asked for the manager and the waiter. The owner went to the door and called me. The police officer looked at me and asked, "Do you remember serving a young white woman here tonight?"

He described the woman. I told him no, I could not recall her. He said to the owner, "its okay. She said the waiter was an old man. This boy is not as old as she is." The girl was eighteen, intoxicated, and was involved in an automobile accident. The police officer was trying to find the person responsible for serving her the alcohol. I remember thinking about how she was older than I was, and yet they showed no concern that I was working in such an establishment even though I was well under the age of twenty-one.

Back to my father, he would often make negative comments about my going to school. He often said, "You should be out working." Not once did he attend any school function while I was in school. The first time I saw him on the school ground was the day I graduated from high school. He made a comment at the graduation ceremony that really confused me. He stated to one of the other parents, "I'm glad to see him finish. It was hard getting him through school." I thought, *that's a strange statement to make.*

In my senior year of high school, I gained the nerve and confidence to challenge my father's behavior. I remember distinctively the first time I challenged his actions. It was one morning as I was coming out of the bathroom preparing for school. He said something I didn't hear. As I walked down the hallway, he started toward me with his hand drawn back. I turned around and said to him, "I think I'm old enough to talk to." He stopped and just looked at me and then walked away.

Many times after that day, I would talk to him about the things he did and said to me. On many occasions, he would sit or stand without answering, and on several occasions, tears came into his eyes. Amazingly, though, not once did he ever say "I am sorry," nor did he ever say "I love you." After high school, I stayed around for a year before being inducted into the army. But before we get into that stage of my life, let me share with you what these experiences taught me.

Again, this is for fathers young and old, rich or poor, of all nationalities. My message is confusing, I know. I'm telling you of the terrible things my father did to me and yet saying that he was a good man. The older I become and the more life experiences I have, the more convinced I am that he *was* a good man. He was a troubled man with many problems, but he was a good man.

There were several times when, after my father would make one of his obnoxious comments to me, he would later do something positive in an attempt to rectify the comments or situation. Fathers, this is okay if the child is able to cope through the formative years and survive to reach an age whereby he or she can analyze our conduct. However, we should do everything possible to never place our children in a position of questioning our love for them.

Throughout my adolescent years, I questioned my father's love; it's a terrible feeling to have to do that. There are several important things a father should do with and for his children. Being there for the child is one of the most important. I know it's impossible for all fathers to physically live in the same household with their children. However, we can make sure our children know that we love them by telling them, encouraging them, and instilling into them that they are very special and precious in our lives.

We must not be afraid to tell them that we love them. We must make every effort possible to communicate with them. We must let them know that we believe in them and trust that they can accomplish any goal they set for themselves. Most important of all is talk with them, encourage them, and never speak to them in a humiliating way. Men, young and old, I'm sharing the history of my relationship with my father as I appeal to you to help change the conditions among far too many of our families.

The one thing I want to be perfectly clear about is that each of us is responsible for our actions. Any dreams I have accomplished were accomplished because I chose to go after them. The things that I failed to do were because I failed, not because of my parents.

We must take responsibility for our actions. Sure, many of us have had tremendous difficulties in our lives while growing up. Many of us face difficult challenges daily in our lives today. If we are to ever succeed in anything, we must face our challenges head-on. It's good to recognize the contributing factors to our challenges. But individually we must mentally and physically address and deal with the obstacles and challenges we face in life.

As a youngster growing up and walking those dirt roads to school, school buses would pass us. They traveled at speeds that forced us to jump across the ditches in an attempt to avoid getting dust blown over us. If it was raining, we had to jump the ditches to avoid getting mud splashed over us. Those buses transported white children to school. Black children had to walk to school. Many of you can perhaps imagine the amazement I felt in the late 1960s and '70s regarding the uproar after the federal courts declared busing to be legal for transporting children to integrated schools. For many years, I had seen buses used for segregation. As a black child, other black children and I were intentionally chased off dirt roads by buses without any consideration for our safety.

These things hurt me then, and even today, the memories are unpleasant as they are for many others. Fathers, we must work diligently to ensure that every child in America has the opportunity of fairness and never feels less than any other child. Years later, I grew to understand that many white people were concerned about my safety as I walked those roads. Many cared deeply about my safety and concerns. They had to live within their culture. As a child, I didn't understand these things. As an adult, I came to understand them. I've also come to understand that we as a human race are one, and each needs the other, regardless of what nationality we are. We must reach out to one another and really attempt to live together without any resentment toward one another.

Today, many of the schools of our inner cities are as segregated as they were when I was a young child growing up. Many of our schools are nothing more than training facilities for gangs and drug pushers. I spoke of my father not going to any of my school activities until the day I graduated from high school. To me, that was wrong. After I became an adult, I told him this. I explained how disappointed it made me feel that he showed no interest until the day I graduated.

Years later, I returned home on vacation during the school year, and he was attending a high school football game. I was slow preparing to go, and he was excited that we were going to miss the kickoff. I mentioned this to my mother, and she informed me that he attended most football games when he was in town. She also said that my talks with him about my feelings about the things that had happened between us had really affected him, and he had made every effort possible not to do those things with the younger siblings. She said that he had even attended Parent-Teacher Association meetings with her. This was the first time to my knowledge that I actually started working toward trying to understand my father.

Today, as I read and hear of the awful conditions in many of our urban schools, I feel a sense of sadness. America can send a man to the moon and *safely* return him to Earth. We are able to place spacecrafts into orbit that can give an individual or vehicle's location within meters. We have the greatest technology of any nation on earth, yet we have far too many children failing to get an adequate education. The sadness I feel comes from what I believe to be a lack of fortitude on behalf of many citizens living within these urban areas.

Not only do I feel sadness that many of the citizens of these areas lack the courage to organize themselves, but they also fail to challenge their elected officials and community leaders to improve their educational systems. Many of these citizens will devote much time and money to purchasing expensive clothing and automobiles from merchants in those communities who prey on them for their livelihood without contributing anything back into their community.

Years ago, when I spoke with my father about my concerns of him not attended any function at my school until I graduated; it apparently had an effect on him. Today, many fathers of those communities with dilapidated schools need someone with the courage to bring them together to change these schools.

A Father's First Obligation

Fathers, our first obligation is to our own flesh and blood. Let us never willingly be removed from our child's life as this child grows in its formative years. There are many men who have walked away from their children because life is or was difficult for them. There are women who have removed their children from their fathers' lives because of hurt, disappointment, or troubles with the father. Numerous families in America have been separated because of divorces. This is understandable; people grow apart or discover that they were not compatible and cannot live together.

If we were fortunate enough to be blessed with the gift of bringing a new life into this world together, we should feel blessed and happy to share in raising that life to maturity. Many move on with another companion; this is the way it should be. However, we should always remember that we share a precious gift with those with whom we were blessed to have a child.

We have an obligation to assist in caring for the child we share together. Mothers, if you are in the position of hating your child's father for whatever you feel he has done to you, please don't make your child suffer his loss in his or her formative years. If the father is unworthy of the child's love and respect, he will demonstrate it to the child. Remember that all children grow to become adults and see things from their perspectives.

Our children today need all the assistance they can possibly get. As we look around us, we see homelessness, hunger, and children in the slum areas of our cities. They need all of our help, particularly the parents who are responsible for their entry into this world. This was one of the biggest lessons I learned from my father. It took me years of growing to realize the significance of his struggles in raising thirteen children under adverse conditions—under conditions, in fact, that were downright atrocious. He stayed there with his children and did the best he could.

Over the years, I have come to understand why he took much of his frustration out on me. I was his oldest child. He had moved away from the harshness of a sharecropper's life to the city and found a job. There he met a young woman, they fell in love, became involved sexually, and I was the result of their sexual involvement. Both were young; she a senior in high school, and he was twenty years old. To do what they thought was right; they married and returned back to the life my father knew so that he could survive with a new family.

Every time things became difficult for him and he saw me, I reminded him of things he wanted to forget. I had nothing to do with his or my mom's conditions. He knew this, and he also knew he had an obligation to try to make life as good as possible for me. That is the reason he was there for me—it's as simple as that. But there was much more I learned about him over the years that I will share with you.

Fathers, lead by teaching the way. Much wisdom lies within our heads. Look around—we have problems. If we refuse to stand with our family, who will? This was another lesson my father taught me. He never spoke the words; I learned this through experience. He was there; he did the best he could. I understand how hard it is for many of our young men today.

Young men, learn from your elders. Study and analyze them. Use the traits that are appealing to you—disregard those that are not. Don't disregard the person, be they relatives or persons unknown. Learn from what you consider are their mistakes.

To my white fathers, history is what it is among our races. Please don't feel my message is not for you. I realize the important and positive contributions you have made toward all the good within my life and the lives of others. I also address you as fathers, and I ask you, whether or not all of our children have paid a high enough price for a history that has not benefitted our nation.

Collectively, are we not better off in this country today than we would be in any other? Are we not all better off when we openly communicate and work together? Do not the same illnesses that affect my child also affect yours? When natural disasters occur, do they only affect my family, not yours, and me? I'm going to be asking fathers many questions throughout this book because; fathers, you and I have an obligation to this country as well as to our families. Moms, I have many questions within my mind for you. However, I can't address you because I don't know how to empathize with your experiences.

My white fathers, many of you have been and are friends of mine. Over the years, several have become my closest friends. We have discussed many issues, agreeing and disagreeing, and those that have come to know me know that I will gladly express my opinions freely as I see them. Many of you have done the same with me. There are many others from races and cultures all over the world with whom I have been associated, many of whom I consider as friends. I ask that men join me. Let's be fathers and teach our younger generations. I know many of you are great fathers and responsible citizens; it's important that we set the example. I believe that we teach by example, not only by lecture. This is another lesson I learned from my father.

Many of us, our fathers, grandfathers, and forefathers, have served this nation in combat. Many of our sons, grandsons, daughters, and granddaughters are serving in combat today. Are we building a nation that follows its creed? Fathers, we have ownership to 50 percent of every decision that is made in our lives. We have 100 percent control over the instrument that allows us to make that decision. Our mind, the other 50 percent, goes to the person we are dealing with.

To the fathers in jail, I'll be expressing my limited experience with many of your conditions. I'll devote a segment of this book to asking you questions—questions that I would like for you to ask yourself and for which I hope you seek honest answers. All I can do is explain my observations, having not lived in or under your conditions.

As I turn back to me and my experiences, I ask as you read this book to keep in mind that I grew up in rural Georgia, a beautiful state. We had no electricity for the first seven or eight years of my life. Maybe it's one of the reasons I'm one of thirteen children. When I was approximately twelve years of age, my parents finally moved away from sharecropping. They moved close to a small college town; the college is now known as Georgia Southern. My father worked at the college caring for the livestock.

That was the first time I recall enjoying school. Years later, I still have fond memories of that school. It was the one school that made learning enjoyable for me. The town is Statesboro, Georgia, and the school was Williams James. Statesboro was the first town I got to see daily. Therefore, I understand my having fond memories of it. As I reflect back to those days at Williams James, I have often thought of the school as being a good school, maybe because it was in a small college town. This perception I have of the school could be wrong, for I was a young child, but as I remember, those days they were pleasant times for me.

Growing Up and Attending School in Savannah

My parents' next move was to Savannah, Georgia, a very beautiful and charming city. It is a city I didn't see the charm in until many years later, after having visited many different cities over the world. I'll address this later, but for now, I want to return to my parents' move to Savannah.

Accurately speaking, this was their return to Savannah; they met in Savannah. My mother had moved to Savannah at a younger age to attend high school. My father had moved to Savannah in his late teens seeking employment away from the sharecroppers' farms.

They met and started a love affair. My mother became pregnant with me; they married and moved back to Screven County to be around their parents. Many years later, I gained a deep appreciation for their desire to make a better life for themselves. As I was growing up, neither parent ever sat with me and explained the difficulties they were facing. Maybe they were trying to protect me. I can't answer the reason they didn't.

I mentioned earlier that I learned to cultivate crops, plowing the fields with a mule. I also learned how to cultivate using a tractor, and this was before I was ten years of age. I mention it now because when my parents returned to Savannah, they rented a house on five acres of land. This house was about a quarter of a mile outside the city limits of Savannah, in a place that later became Garden City.

Within that quarter of a mile, between the city limit of Savannah and the land my parents rented, was a small community of homes occupied by black Americans. Every street within that community was dirt, and many of the houses were little more than shacks. There were several little gangs. They were not violent in the sense that they were killing each other, but there were fistfights, although they were few.

After moving into our new house, my father bought a mule and plow. He started a vegetable farm on the five acres, and I spent many hours plowing and tending to that farm. Many of the boys my age would tease me about being a farmer. My father would hire me out to cultivate small plots of land for other people who wanted vegetable gardens. To me, this was humiliating. I was fourteen or fifteen years old in a new environment and at an easily impressionable age trying to fit in. The young fellows my age from the neighborhood would announce at school that I was a farmer and that I often plowed with a mule after school. This statement was true. However, it had a negative connotation to me. To me, the statement said, "If you are a farmer, you are not as good as we are."

Fathers, believe me, years later, I appreciated the lessons I learned from plowing with that mule and working the five-acre plot of land. After becoming an adult, I realized that the farm provided a means of adequate nourishment for my family. My father could not farm the garden. Most of his time was spent away from home trying to provide for his family. He had gotten employment as a long-distance truck driver for a moving company, and he was gone for days at a time. There were times when he would be at home for only a couple of days before he would be gone again. When he was there, he would help me with the farm and teach me different ways to work the farm. As I reflect back on that period of my childhood, I now realize that they were good years. I didn't understand them then, and this is another reason I am sharing a part of my life story. Had my father known how much it would have meant to sit me down and explain the reasons he had me doing those things, I think he would have done so.

We must carefully develop young minds. Feeding our children information in a loving manner and listening to them closely greatly improves their chances of becoming productive citizens. Throughout this book, I will make references to fathers. Young men who are not fathers, I am speaking to you also. I sincerely hope that something in this writing will make a positive influence on someone's life.

As we talk with our children, we must not let the frustrations of our life struggles be directed at them in a negative manner. Earlier, I mentioned many of the cruel things my father would say to me when I did something he didn't approve of. As I grew older, experience and observations of his actions taught me that many times I had done nothing he disapproved of. He would be facing some personal crisis, and I was available for him to vent his frustrations on.

Men, we must not under any circumstances allow the negative conditions within our lives to cause us to place them on our children. If things are difficult, be the reasons financial or medical, sit your child down and talk *with* him or her, not *to* him or her. I emphasize talking *with* instead of *to* him or her. I can't stress enough the importance of being a presence in children's lives. Fathers, I'm not asking that you talk with your sons, but with your sons and daughters. Be honest and be sincere, as they can comprehend much more, than we give them acknowledgment for.

On our arrival in Savannah, I enrolled in Woodsville Secondary School. To the best of my recollection, I was in the eighth grade. The children from the neighborhood were not that friendly in the beginning. The families within the immediate vicinity of our house were terrific. None of them had young boys; my dilemma was establishing a friendship with young boys. The few girls, who live close, were friendly and chivalrous towards my siblings and me.

Looking back over the years, I have mixed emotions about Woodsville School and many of its teachers. Many of the good days of my early life were spent there. Several of my teachers were dedicated in trying to prepare their students for the future under abysmal conditions. As I entered the ninth grade, Woodsville High School burned down. The elementary, secondary, and high school students had to share facilities. This continued until I was in my senior year of high school. During those years, I gave no serious thought to all grades sharing the same facilities. I lived under a segregated system, one that demonstrated a mode of behavior which said that I was not as good as white people were or as worthy of an education as the white children were.

I grew up in an atmosphere that said if you were "colored," you were an inferior person. It was years later that I really understood the significance of the lack of educational training I received at Woodsville, later renamed Sophronia Tompkins High School. This was a sad period in the history of our country. We must not look on that period with hate or resentment but learn the lessons it taught. As men and fathers, we must ensure that this never occurs again. Our responsibilities are to learn from past inequities and work hard to see that we don't repeat the same.

Yet, sadly, conditions much worse than those that existed in Savannah and at Sophronia Tompkins High School continued to exist in 1991, thirty-odd years later, as described so eloquently by Jonathan Kozol in his book, *Savage Inequalities: Children in America's Schools.* I feel this book is a must read for all adults. Education is our paramount tool for future preparedness, and we must do much more to improve the educational systems of our inner cities.

Many years ago, I recognized a characteristic about me that I didn't understand. Whenever I was required to take a written test, my test scores would be much lower than my scores would be from a multiple choice test. Years later when I was a freshman in college, my English professor counseled me reference my ability to know the subject well, but could not communicate my knowledge well in written form. He suggested strongly that I remain in college because my knowledge of the subject far exceeded students whose grades was higher than mine because of my writing skills. He said he was convinced that my ability to learn and communicate my knowledge about a subjected far exceeded my lack of writing skills. After graduating if I'm in a position of needing to write professional letters, to get a good secretary and dictate to her.

The above statement hurt. You see, I had made a career in the army, opened and ran a business, but deep within me I knew his statement was true. I mentioned the counseling session to my wife and her comment, "Then your secretary will know more about your business than you, didn't make me feel any better. Therefore I forgot my inability to effectively communicate in writing until I read the book "Bill Clinton-My Life" specifically one paragraph I'm going to paraphrase.

Former President Clinton was talking about a period of his life when he was a law professor at the University of Arkansas law school. He stated an observation he noticed between 1973 and 1976, involving approximately twenty-three black law student. He mentioned one student in particularly he knew had studied and understood the material, yet his answers to the exam didn't show it. He wrote of several such incidents of these students' bad grammar and poor sentence structure. After reading this, I again thought of my English professor counseling session.

This time I asked myself why was I deficient in the above areas? First I thought about this characteristic of my using bad grammar and poor sentence structure. I and many blacks of my period from the south didn't know we were speaking improper language until we were adults. Our language consists of broken parts of whatever culture our ancestors were from and the learning of other languages by sound. Keep in mind my ancestors were forbidden educational training. I thought of my very first school and Mrs. Ida Barnes, can you imagine the difficult task she had trying to teach four grades all combined in a maximum space of 600 square feet or less. America too many children of all races are not getting the necessary training in these skills now.

Growing up in rural Georgia, I cried many days and nights because of things, my father said to me and because of activities within my living environment that I didn't understand. Deep within me, I knew that many things were not right. I didn't know what needed changing or how to change them. I didn't have life experiences or an education upon which to base an evaluation—just a child's limited understanding of the world around him.

There was no television or twenty-four-hour news networks to assist in educating me, only my elders. Fathers and men, we see life from different perspectives. Our children are just beginning their journey through life. In this simple man's opinion, the greatest gift we can give our children is to listen to them. Try to understand the conditions and times they are growing up in and set positive examples for them. Hope and pray that we surround them in an environment that teaches the values we believe in.

Again, my comments and beliefs are of one man's experiences in our Unites States of America; these experiences are seen through the eyes of one black man. I sincerely hope that these experiences have not obscured my ability to intelligently evaluate situations and conditions and act accordingly.

Over the years, my experiences have been a valuable asset and teaching tool for me. One of those lessons learned from my experiences is that race and ethnicity problems have caused many of the ill effects from which our nation suffers. We are all members of the human race. We are Americans, and what affects one of us eventually affects each of us, not always directly, but indirectly and many times in minuscule ways.

This writing is about a few of my experiences in America, the best country I have lived in or have visited in my lifetime so far. I have a great love for this country and desire the best for all our citizens. This is why this book is my personal plea to everyone who reads it. Help make it a great country for all our citizens. My belief is that the first and best place to start this process is with our children. As I see it, they are our future, and if we desire this future to be bright and glorious, we must invest the money, time, and energy in making it so.

My First Real Education

Woodsville—later known as Sophronia Tompkins High School—provided somewhat of an educational foundation for me. My education really began after my induction into the United States Army in June of 1960. I began to mature in a manner that was interesting and disappointing. My first few months going through basic training and advanced training were very rewarding.

For the first time in my life, I was equal to everyone around me. If there were prejudices towards the races it was not openly displayed amongst the cadre, everyone was treated the same. That experience was very impressive and gratifying. While in basic training, I met a couple of young White men who befriended me.

One of the men was from Gainesville, Florida. I will not name any of these individuals out of respect for their privacy. I'll never forget this young man and many others I'll mention throughout this book. They made tremendously favorable impressions on my life, and I thank them. After basic training, my first duty station was Fort Lewis, Washington. I was assigned to a unit that had some extreme radical racists in it. These men were young junior leaders. They had no reservation against using the *N*-word in front of a black person if that person was alone among them.

We eventually got a black commander. I requested permission to see him and was denied permission. In those days, there was no such thing as an "Open Door Policy" where a soldier could report to the commander's office at a given time. The soldier was required to go through his chain of command, and my chain of command had refused my request. It was customary for units to have a full field layout inspection on Saturday mornings. Commanders would often walk through on Friday nights while their units were preparing for the next morning's inspection.

One Friday night the commander came through with his subordinate leaders following him. When he came into my cubicle I requested permission to report to his office to speak with him. His reply was, "Come through your chain of command like all other soldiers. My chain of command was traveling with him. I informed him I had tried and was told I could not see him. You should have seen the expressions on their faces as they were standing behind him and heard the entire conversation.

The commander turned and looked at them without saying anything; he turned to me and said, "Meet me at my office in five minutes." I went to his office and informed him of blatant incidents of racism that I had witnessed without any attempt from them of concealing their feelings. What action he took I don't know however, their behavior changed. The reason I mention this incident is because it reminds me, that regulations can be put into place to protect and assist us however, without the knowledge, willingness and courage to confront adverse conditions, laws and regulations will not help us.

Before continuing with my military experiences, let me share some of my enjoyable experiences of attending Woodsville (later Sophronia Tompkins High School). Although I was not an outstanding student, getting good grades was not difficult for me. I had a very good memory. If I saw the teacher do it, I could easily remember how to do it. I was not one of the popular guys on campus. However, I had no difficulty in relationships with the young women at school. Years later, I learned the students called me a loner, because I associated with no group, and treated the young women with respect.

Most people meet someone of the opposite sex who greatly influences his or her life; with me, it was no exception. I met a beautiful young black woman in the tenth grade. She was one of the school's majorettes. We dated steadily for a period, but eventually we started dating others. We remained friends through high school and until after my introduction into the army.

This young woman was the first of the opposite sex who taught me that men and women could remain terrific friends even while and after dating other people. I later met a young woman in my senior year of high school who I would eventually marry. Again, I learned much from this woman. I'll not name her out of respect for her privacy, but she taught me many lessons.

In her younger years, she was as beautiful as any Miss America was. She was a total joy to be with, and look at. We first met as I was walking home one evening. She entered the street from a connecting street in front of me. After seeing her, I quickened my pace trying to catch up with her, however she sped up. We reached my house, and as I turned into the driveway, I said, "Good evening," she replied, "Good evening." I went into the house not knowing who she was, but remembering her.

Several days later, one evening, I went to the grocery store, which was about three blocks from our house, and this young woman was in the store. I got the items I went after, went outside, and waited on her. It was raining, and I was glad it was. She came out of the store, and I asked if I could give her a ride home. She accepted. As I was driving her home, I learned that she had a sister in one of my classes at school. I knew her parents and two of her brothers. After talking for a while, I asked if I could see her again on a date. She accepted my invitation, and we started dating.

This young woman's parents were wealthy compared to the other blacks in their neighborhood. Her father was self-employed, owned several houses, and drove a new Cadillac. We got along great together. She would often visit me at my parents' home, and my parents loved her. Her parents and I had always gotten along well prior to my knowing her. In fact, her father treated me as a son prior to my dating his daughter. Why I had not met her prior to the night at the store I don't know. I had met her older sister and the one who was in one of my classes. Anyway, we dated steadily until my induction into the army in June 1960. Afterwards we wrote and continued our love affair until the summer of 1961, when we decided to marry.

We married in June 1961. She joined me in Washington in January 1962. This was one of the happiest periods of my life. We enjoyed being around each other and doing things together. We had a wonderful time in Washington until June 1962, which was the end of my obligation in the military. She and several of our friends and acquaintances thought I should stay in the military. I was adapting to military life fairly well, and we were having the time of our lives.

Therefore, I reenlisted, and we went to Fort Ord, California. We continued to have the time of our lives. In November of 1962, I received orders for Germany. This was okay with the both of us. We left Fort Ord. She went to Savannah to stay with her parents, and I went to Germany. After arriving in Germany in late January 1963, I put a request in to have my wife join me. The army approved my request, and she joined me in May 1963.

Prior to graduating high school, in my senior year, I worked part time for a moving and storage company. After graduating,

I worked for this company full time. The pay was not great, but it allowed me to assist my parents and have money for dating. Furthering my education was not a priority. In fact, I neither saw possibility nor gave any serious thought of going to college.

Many would say that I had no ambition. Looking back today, I would agree with them. However, at the time, living from day to day in an impoverished, segregated community was an accomplishment within itself. Poverty is demoralizing to a young person's psyche and especially to those not provided an adequate early education.

Good early childhood education is essential for one to dream of expanding their possibilities in life. Not only does a good early childhood education assist in building dreams, it prepares a child for future learning. As I reflect back to those years, my actions and ambitions were identical to those of the other young men of my community. Our major ambition was to survive the best way we could from day to day.

Fathers, there are several of you who understand the above feeling of trying to survive from day to day. I am asking those who have survived and succeeded in making a better life for themselves to please go back into our economically depressed communities and talk with the young men in them today. Offer encouragement; share our knowledge and life lessons. Perhaps if enough of us share information of our struggles, and how we succeeded, some of our young people will find something to help them to succeed.

Back to the beginning of my military service, as stated earlier, my basic and advanced training was a new experience. I was born into a segregated system in the Deep South of Georgia. I grew up in a segregated system and knew nothing else. As a very young child, I was taught to be subservient to the white man and not to challenge anything he said. Worse than not to challenge anything he said was to tolerate his disrespect for my mother and sisters.

Emphases were placed on my highly respecting the Caucasian women. Often my father and elders reminded me, to never speak or say anything to one, unless she spoke to me, and then be cautious with my response. All Black males my age from the South, knew the Emmet Till story well; it was imbedded into our mind. Emmett Till was a fourteen-year-old black who was brutally beaten and murdered; his body weighted down with an iron cotton gin wheel and dumped into the Tallahatchie River in Mississippi, for speaking to a white woman.

As a child growing up, I knew this philosophy was wrong and rebelled against it on several occasions. My rebellious behavior caused my parents concern many times. However, I never pushed issues to the point of having difficulties with the local authorities. The sensation of relief experienced immediately after entering the army soon vanished to be replaced by the reality that racism was alive and thriving in the army.

On arriving at Fort Lewis Washington, in the fall of 1960, I was assign to a platoon with several southern Whites in it. Several of those men had no reservations of reminding Black's they were unwelcome, and the only reason for tolerating blacks and other minorities was, integration was the Department of Defense Policy. Once sunset came or once one was off duty, their association was with their ethnic group.

Several young black soldiers fought this on-duty discrimination by addressing the matter with their chains of command. Others fought by studying, learning their jobs, and performing their duties more so than their White contemporaries. Our emphases were to obtain promotion and place ourselves in a position to apply the regulations equally to everyone

To obtain promotion, often black and minority soldiers' duty performance had to be superior to our White contemporary; this included performing the simplest of tasks. In those days' soldiers performed tasks such as (kp) Kitchen Police. Duties included operating the dishwasher, peeling potatoes, cleaning the grease traps, cleaning pots and pans, food line servers, and-serving-as-dining waiters for the commissioned officers.

Another such example was guard duty, this required walking around motor pools and empty buildings. The soldier most knowledgeable and neatly dressed would be selected Colonel's Orderly. The Colonel Orderly's duty was to run errands for the Colonel. To be selected Colonel's Orderly were considered to be a privilege and honor.

My referring to the above duties as simple tasks does not mean they were not important tasks. Obviously, for health reasons kitchen police were an extremely important duty. Cleaning the grease trap was the duty all soldiers dreaded, yet cleaning it was very important for health and sanitation reason. There was a vast amount of information learned about ones military specialty while preparing to compete for Colonels Orderly. Walking guard duty around empty buildings and motor pools taught obedience to orders and how to do the simple things right.

The times were not great for black men. However, they were better in the military than on most jobs in the civilian market. This was in the early 1960s, and the Equal Rights Amendment had not yet become law.

It was on my first assignment to Fort Lewis, Washington, and residing in Tacoma that I first became involved with children labeled as Youth-at-Risk. I met an army chief warrant officer who often visited my next-door neighbor, who was a non-commissioned officer in my unit. We played cards regularly. The non-commissioned officer and his wife had seven children. This chief warrant officer talked to me about becoming the Scout Master of a Boy Scout Troop, which was in need of a Scout Master.

The chief warrant officer was between forty and forty-five years old and I was twenty-one. He would bring the subject-up of my taking the scoutmasters' position, each time he saw me.

His persuasive argument was; he had observed my interactions with my neighbor's children and their affection for me. After a short period of persuasion, he convinced me to become the scoutmaster. He assisted with the paperwork and arranged for me to attend a few classes to familiarize myself with the duties of a Scout Master.

Initially, the boys and I didn't hit it off well. They were mischievous and disobedient of rules. Maybe this disobedience was because I was a young man. Many of them were attending the meetings simply because their moms made them go. Several of them had no fathers present in their lives.

My first couple of months with the Boy Scout troop was challenging. Several of the boys demonstrated destructive and rebellious behavior; others were mischievous and disobedient. After talking with and encouraging them, within a couple of months, several started to change their attitudes, wanting to become involved. Many would visit my house, spending their spare time on Saturday and Sunday afternoons. Why did these children accept me and my wife? At that time, I didn't know or think much about it other than we were both young adults, had no children, and enjoyed spending time with them.

Years later, I know why they accepted us. We showed an interest in them as individuals. My wife would often serve popcorn, hot dogs, and juice when they visited. We made them feel that we cared. Some came from one-parent families and had no positive male role model in their lives. Their mothers didn't have time to dedicate to them. Many mothers were working in restaurants and nightclubs and had other children with limited time to share. When not on duty, my wife and I were available. To some of them, we became surrogate parents.

In June of 1962, we departed Tacoma, for my new assignment at Fort Ord, California. On arriving in California at Fort Ord, I saw that Southern Georgia was not the only state with racial problems. Seaside, the small town closest to

Fort Ord, exhibited an attitude of not caring for blacks, either. Seaside also was my first introduction to behavior displayed toward Mexican Americans, which was the same as what was displayed toward blacks, in my opinion.

My stay at Fort Ord was short. Six months after my arrival, I was assign to Germany. On arriving in Germany, I was assign to the tank section of a platoon in Troop A, First Squadron, Fourteenth Armored Cavalry Regiment in Fulda, Germany. I arrived at the unit approximately eight in the morning. Before lunch, I was on the east-west German border for a week. Shortly after returning from the border, I was deployed to another small camp for a week.

Immediately after returning from that deployment, my leaders chose me to deploy early, as a member of the advance party, to the largest live fire training range in West Germany. The squadron was deploying there for a month of live fire training. By that time, I had been promoted to the rank of a noncommissioned officer. Shortly after returning to Fulda my wife joined me.

That duty assignment was challenging, particularly the first few months. It was because I was selected to lead a tank section without having prior experience with tanks. Some of the men had more years in the military and tank units than I. A couple of the soldiers held the same pay grade as I, one had more years in our pay grade than I had in the military, they were specialist, and I was a Sergeant.

Learning the job was challenging and rewarding. I had the privilege of working with the best platoon sergeant I saw during my twenty-two-year military career. He was a white man from Kansas. He had a brother serving with the Fourteenth Armored Cavalry Regiment; he was the regiment rations noncommissioned officer. The regiment rations noncommissioned officer managed and operated the Regiment dining facilities this included requisitioning rations.

If that platoon sergeant had prejudices, he did not display them. He was honest, sincere, and dedicated. That soldier gained my loyalty, trust and total respect. Throughout my military career and life, I have valued my experiences with this man. It was also in this unit that I met another young white noncommissioned officer of the same rank as I. I gained tremendous respect and affection for this man. This man was from Marietta, Georgia. He would visit my home often, bringing flowers to my wife. Often he would go into our kitchen without saying anything to us and commence cooking as if he were at home.

It was while assigned to this squadron that education became important to me. I began to read constantly. Much of my reading was dedicated to military manuals, learning as much as possible about armored cavalry. This was my first genuine realization that education offered real, tangible benefits. People can espouse education as loudly and as often as they like. However, it means very little or nothing to the great majority of children living in city ghettos and attending schools that are overcrowded with outdated books and unqualified teachers who really don't want to be there teaching.

As stated earlier, a couple of the soldiers in the tank section had many more years of military service than I did. Some held the same pay grade with more time in that pay grade than I had in service. The distinctive difference between them and me was that I was promoted as a noncommissioned officer, and they were specialists. Noncommissioned officers outranked specialists.

Why had I been promoted as an NCO? At the time, I had no idea. I knew that I attempted to perform my duties in a professional manner. I was willing to read and learn everything possible about my duties. My superiors recognized this dedication and selected me to attend what was then considered to be one of the army's best noncommissioned officers' development schools. I graduated from this school within the top ten. This created a sense within me that I could compete and do well. I graduated from the Seventh Army Noncommissioned Officer Academy on November 23, 1963, the day President John F. Kennedy was assassinated.

My friend from Marietta, Georgia, and I would often go to a German club or the NCO club for entertainment, and often my wife would accompany us. I returned to the United States and Fort Lewis, Washington, he was assigned there later, and we continued our friendship. Often, if my wife and I had an engagement and could not find a babysitter on short notice, he would offer to babysit. This man and the previous two mentioned white men gave me my first truly favorable appreciation of the white race.

There were a few occasions in Germany when I ran across what I considered racism. Once was at a troop noncommissioned officers' party, held at one of the local nightclubs. The troop's entire noncommissioned officers cadre and their wives were at this nightclub. My wife and I were dancing, as were many other couples, and the dance floor was crowded. My Platoon Sergeant, who replaced the previous one mentioned grasp my wife's butt.

She slapped the hell out of him there on the dance floor. Several people saw or heard her slap him. Neither they nor I had seen him grasp her. After she slapped him, she told me what had occurred. I was prepared to defend her honor. Fortunately for everyone, he left the dance floor, and she and I continued to dance. As stated earlier, this woman was a beautiful woman. She grew up relatively wealthy compared to most blacks in her neighborhood and was not intimidated by racism.

This platoon sergeant came to me the Monday morning following the incident and apologized. He said he had drank too much, and was sorry for his behavior. Several thoughts ran through my mind. First, he had insulted my wife's dignity as she danced in the arms of her husband. Second, he had such disregard for me as a man; that he felt at liberty to disrespect and disgrace my wife, in my presence. Had a black man done that, would my assumption have been it was because of our race? Truthfully, I'm doubtful that I would have thought so. Would I have been angry? Yes, very much so, and I know I would have taken the same pleasure from her reaction.

Why did I infer this man's behavior as racial motivated? It was because actions of such nature were commonly perpetuated against blacks. However, through the years, I have come to realize that all races have ignorant people. This man's actions could have been influenced by the amount of alcohol he had consumed. However, in those days, because of my exposure to segregation, poverty, and hostile conditions, my first thoughts were racist.

Think of the child today—the one who doesn't know where his or her father or mother is, or whose parents are living in rat-infested ghetto neighborhoods, those who are homeless or going to dilapidated schools. When unpleasant incidents occur within the lives of these children, can they rationally interpret them? One's ability to think rationally is greatly impeded when living under deplorable conditions.

My friend and I discussed the above incident and came to the same conclusions. The incident was wrong, it was demeaning, and it hurt my wife to the extent that she reacted hostilely without thinking. Had this man said anything or reacted to her response in a negative manner, it could have destroyed my military career because I was prepared to defend her dignity. We also concluded that the military would have defended this man. He was of superior rank to me, and no one saw him grasp her. This may not have been true, but my white friend and I came to those conclusions. This was because of our environment.

My wife became pregnant shortly after arriving in Germany. We were ecstatic and looked forward to the birth of our child. Our first child together was a boy; we were both excited and overjoyed. During this period, I was deployed on maneuvers regularly. Very seldom was I at home for more than a week at a time. In fact, before our son was born, my superiors thought it was time that I attend the Noncommissioned Officer Academy. I discussed this with my wife. She agreed, saying, "Go now; the baby is not due yet." We were both pleased that I was progressing in the military without difficulty.

My First Realization of Maturing as a Man

We traveled around West Germany discovering and enjoying the sites. Our son was born on February 9, 1964. I was on guard duty the night she gave birth. I would leave my duty station and go home between shifts to ensure that she was okay. The second time I went home, she was in labor. We went to the little dispensary at Downs Barracks, Fulda, Germany, where we were stationed.

The doctor sent her back home, saying she was not ready. I went back to duty and returned two hours later to hear her moaning as I walked up the walkway to the house. I rushed in and assisted her to the car, and we rushed to the dispensary. The doctor again said she was not ready. I asked him if he was aware that she was having a Caesarian section. He answered no, went to check her record, came back, and said, "We need to get her to Frankfurt within an hour." He called for a helicopter and was inform that it would take some time to locate a crew to fly the helicopter.

He then informed me that our baby would have to be delivered at the local German hospital in Fulda. We rushed to the hospital, and as soon as we arrived, we were met by a group of nuns. The nuns took charge; approximately thirty minutes later, one of the nuns came to me and said, "It's a boy." This was the happiest day of my life to that point. My wife and son stayed in the hospital for approximately three weeks. The day after they came home from the hospital, I had to deploy for thirty days on a field exercise.

In defense of the doctor who was on duty at the dispensary who sent my wife home, he was German and filling in for the American doctor. It was early in the morning, and he was not familiar with her history. He gave her a quick physical exam without checking her record, a negligence mistake, one that caused my wife a substantial amount of pain and anxiety. My anxiety began the moment the doctor said, we must get her to Frankfurt within an hour. Until that moment, my concerns had been at a minimum. At that moment, my concerns drastically increased.

This was the ninth of February in Germany; it's approximately fifty miles from Fulda to Frankfurt, at least an hour drive on a clear day, now he tells me, we have less than an hour to get my wife there, on snow and icy roads. Remember, I was on guard duty, as a commander of relief, going home every two hours. There were several factors surrounding that incident that displeased us. However, we were grateful for the results, a healthy son, without physical damage to mother or son. The doctor's mistake was a negligent mistake, however an understandable mistake.

There were racial incidents that happened in the United States, during my assignment in Germany, many of which tore to the soul of my being. Those incidents hurt me. The depth of my hurt is hard to explain. Imagine being in a foreign country in the armed forces of your country and seeing policemen using clubs, horses, water hoses, and police dogs brutalizing your ethnic group, all because they wanted their rights as human beings—rights guaranteed to us as citizens of the United States by our Constitution. Many black Americans had fought in the two world wars and in Korea. Many were serving in Germany, as I was, to protect the Germans' rights to live freely. Seeing my people brutalized by the people who were responsible for protecting them was humiliating and disgraceful.

It was a dreadful feeling knowing those actions were wrong and not being in a position to do anything about it. Laws that were supposed to protect you were working against you. Who does one turn to for help? Unless one has lived in the conditions, it is very difficult if not impossible to explain the mentality of the person living in those conditions.

Any man of worth could not avoid questioning his decisions seeing the events that were taking place within the United States on Germany's news media each evening. It was during this period that I began to study Dr. Martin Luther King Jr. and tried to understand his teachings of nonviolence. To be completely honest, I couldn't comprehend the philosophy. I had much hurt and anger. I knew that there was little I could do to change the situation at home in the United States. My only option was to be a good soldier and to speak out to those of equal or superior ranks to protect soldiers subordinate in rank and to ensure we were treated equally.

Those years provided important learning experiences for me, but many of the lessons were confusing. How to relate to others as humans was bewildering to me. We were told every day what a great country we lived in and how just our laws were for all citizens. During that period, I was a young black man with a high school education—an education which was not of the best quality. I had graduated from a segregated school where the secondary and high school youngsters had to use the same facility for most of my high school years. This was because the high school had burned down in my freshman year.

Our books and learning materials were passed down from the white schools as they updated their learning materials. I began to educate myself, not by attending formal educational programs, but by reading different books on subjects of interest to me. Far too many of America's youths today are without adequate school materials to provide them the education they'll need to survive successfully in an electronic and computerized society. Many children are dropping out of school prior to finishing the twelfth grade. We can improve these conditions. More financial aid could help in many of our economically depressed communities, but there are other ways to help. For example, through individual voluntary contributions, we can gather our youths and tutor them in the skills and trades they'll require.

This requires a small amount of effort, but the returns from this effort are great. Let me share a story with you about a former neighbor of mine. This woman had a young daughter who had just started kindergarten. This mother wanted her child to socialize and play with other children after kindergarten in the afternoons. She went to every house within our cul-de-sac talking with mothers who had daughters of the same age. Neighbors with girls approximately the age of her child were asked to allow their child to come to her house at a set time each afternoon. This woman taught these girls using educational games. All of the girls loved going to her house. She entertained her daughter while educating her and the neighbors' girls.

Another method of assisting our children to remain in school is through community organizations, such as schools, churches, fraternities, and social organizations forming alliances. Churches could offer their facilities for use by the community for tutoring youths who are having difficulties in their studies. Many of our social organizations and fraternities have college graduates and teachers educated in the various sciences that can offer their assistance.

It was in Germany that I began to appreciate different cultures by attending and mixing in many of their social activities. One of the most important lessons I learned in Germany was to never prejudge a person or thing. Up to that point in my life, I had no real appreciation for myself as a black person. I had allowed others to dictate who and what I was. A German acquaintance invited me to an African ballet. I refused the invitation, thinking to myself, *why would I want to see a bunch of blacks jumping around?*

This acquaintance purchased the tickets, anyway. I attended the ballet to show my respect. The ballet ignited an excitement within me that I had not experienced until then. Since then, I've seen many ballets and plays. I have come to love the theaters and the arts. Why do I feel that this event merits mentioning? Because over the years, I've seen far too many youths exposed to the same ignorance I was exposed to. Having not been exposed to plays and the arts, my impression of Africans was of them jumping around with sticks as they were portrayed on television.

This period was also the beginning of me trying to learn about myself. I asked myself a lot of questions. Who was I? What did I want out of life? How to better support my family—and what could I do to better myself? My emphasis began to shift to me, particularly whether I was being a good provider for the woman I married and our child. I gained strength and courage from reflecting back to the days when my father had me in those cotton fields and working those farms as he labored hard to provide food and shelter for his family.

The knowledge that my challenges were nothing compared to the challenges my father had endured sustained me. I would not have known this had he not been there for me to observe. Sure, I would have understood the harshness of the conditions I grew up under. I probably would have faulted him for contributing to those conditions had he not been there. Fathers, we are teachers, and in so many ways, we set examples. Maybe for the first time in my life, I began to understand love as I realized that my family's joy and wellbeing were my most important obligation.

Community Involvement

Again, I say "fathers," because to me, fathers are love. Fathers are teachers, and fathers are mentors. Fathers are involved within their communities, either directly or indirectly, positively or negatively, but we are involved. I often compare people to grains of sand and grains of seeds. I will explain this comparison, but first, I would like to address some of the areas in which I believe we need to become more actively involved in a positive way and point out some of the consequences that have occurred through a lack of what I believe to be positive, active involvement.

It should be obvious—first is our children. Fathers, many of us are abandoning our children. In several of our communities, gangs are running rampant, and our citizens are killed walking the streets or sitting within the walls of their homes in what is termed drive-by shootings. I have often asked myself, who are the people committing these crimes? My answer is always the same. They are my neighbors and your neighbors. How we can correct the problems? I believe there are several ways in which we can correct the problems. We start with ourselves, by ensuring our conduct is above reproach. If we are parents, we begin by teaching love, and I believe we teach through demonstrated actions, not words.

We cannot teach our children love if we are constantly arguing or making derogatory remarks about our friends and neighbors. We must establish rules of conduct within our homes and ensure that our children abide by them. Children need and expect discipline, for discipline is the one quality that is necessary to accomplish any goal. Let's not forget respect—respect for themselves, others, and good old responsibility. Each individual must account for his or her actions and accept the fact that he or she has control over his or her actions.

Again, we must teach not through lectures but by demonstration. Not only must we teach our children, we must share this with all children. We must not be afraid to correct unacceptable conduct from children within our community. If they are violating the law, we should call the police. It's our responsibility. If we are adults and see a child erring in his or her ways, we have a responsibility to point this out to the child, for we are the teachers. We often say that gangs have taken over communities. I don't believe that gangs have taken over our communities. I understand gangs are in several of our communities.

The communities in which these gangs are running rampant were given to them. Too many of us refused to become involved. We closed our doors and pretended we were unaware of the activities taking place. We placed bars on our windows and doors to keep people with unacceptable conduct out and then became prisoners within our homes.

Some of us moved to the suburbs to avoid the "bad elements." Guess what? The "bad elements" moved to the suburbs, too; that's where the money is. It seems to me that not being actively involved in a positive manner sends a negative message to our children. We ask them to obey our culture and societal rules, yet they see adults failing to enforce the rules we ask them to obey. I believe that we must teach through demonstrated performance.

In many communities, our schools, instead of providing a safe environment for learning, they have become a place for criminal elements to prey on our young people. Drugs have infiltrated down into our elementary schools. Taking guns to school are an everyday occurrence in many of our school systems. To quote Dante, "The hottest places in hell are reserved for those who, in the times of moral crisis, preserve their neutrality." I believe this issue to be the equivalent of a moral crisis.

What can we do to improve the situation? I believe we start by ensuring that our children don't get these guns at home. We visit our schools, talk with the teachers, and become interested in what is occurring at our schools. Let's establish programs within our communities to keep our young people occupied after school hours and encourage them to participate through our involvement. By doing nothing, we encourage our children to look for alternate means of occupying their minds and expressing their creativity. We must also become members of our school boards and be an effective voice for improvement and cultural inclusion within our schools.

Educating our youths is the most important investment a culture, community, state, or nation can make. I believe it is becoming critical for all voices to be heard. Many of our public educational systems do not appear to be providing the necessary skills required for our children to succeed in the global economy today. Many of our elected officials express their opinions that several of our educational systems are failing but offer no positive solutions for repairing the systems. If you were the owner of a business and employed someone to work for you and all they did was complain about the problems of the job without finding a solution to solve the problems, how long would you employ that person?

It is time that we hold our elected officials accountable for finding adequate solutions to our education problems. We elect individuals to our boards of education—is it not their responsibility to make a serious analysis and evaluation of our educational system and then make recommendations for improvement?

We, the general public, have failed to hold these officials to their duties of providing an adequate education for our children. We have heard many opinions suggesting means of providing a better educational system. Some suggest regional boards of education instead of one system for the entire state. A regional system appears more appealing to me, but I'm one voice. Whether we have regional systems or one system is not important. What's important is that the educational systems prepare our children for the future regardless of what direction our future is headed.

As contributing citizens of our state and nation, we deserve better than we are getting. Many of our public schools are not preparing our children to meet the future employment markets. Several of our schools do not have adequate facilities or teachers with the experience or ability to teach our youths to meet future needs. There are many reasons for this. One is that we don't pay our teachers enough to encourage the best to become the educators of our youths. It has amazed me over the years how much we are willing as a society to pay professional sports players and entertainers to entertain us and yet complain about the amount we are willing to pay to secure our future.

Perhaps it's time to revise our public school systems, especially at the high school level. I suggest that we investigate forming partnerships between the public school systems and private industries. These partnerships could be established in the form of laboratory schools comprised of major industries and institutions, such as the building, automotive, electronic, chemical, educational, and medical industries.

In my opinion, partnerships between public education institutions and private industries benefit everyone concerned. They benefit the various industries and institutions by allowing them direct input into the curriculum being taught, as well as providing a continuous pool of well-trained employees. They benefit the public educational systems by allowing them to educate on specific needs of society and a professional resource of advisors. They benefit the students by allowing them to concentrate on core subjects in their fields of interest.

Communities within close proximity of each other with high schools that are teaching identical subjects could be transformed into laboratory schools, teaching the core curriculum of a specific industry. For example, instead of two high schools in a town—West High School and South High School—teaching identical curricula, they could establish partnerships whereby one teaches only courses directly related to the medical industry and the other teaches only courses related to and needed in the electronic industry. Where possible, each of our high schools should teach core curricula for major industries and institutions. Students should be evaluated and whenever possible encouraged to attend the school that they have the aptitude for and desire to attend.

These laboratory schools should be small, with small class sizes and instruction based on individual achievement. As the students progress, they should be advanced depending on individual attainment. This would eliminate the pressure on some students to learn at a rate that is hectic for them. It also allows for mastery of a particular phase of training before advancing, thereby building self-esteem and confidence in their abilities. Perhaps we need to seriously revaluate what's being taught at our junior colleges

Many industries don't require a college education for employment but do require highly skilled employees. The forming of industry and public education partnerships can provide highly skilled individuals at an early age and a continuous pool of loyal employees. Those industries and institutions that require college-level or advanced-degree educated personnel benefit by those students pursuing careers in those areas and concentrating on their studies by training with students of similar abilities. Instructors are not forced to try to teach students that have no desire or ability to be in their classes. Maybe there are schools of these characteristics already in existence; if so, they should be studied closely and, if successful, copied.

Our youths are our future, and the trend toward future occupations that pays enough to live on requires a college or post-graduate degree and/or highly skilled training. In my opinion, to maintain a middle-class society, we are going to require major changes in our educational system. To affect these changes is going to require all of our involvement. We must become actively involved in every segment of our community and government; we must demand that those responsible for educating our youths educate them for the future. This includes their parents.

As to my statement earlier of often comparing people to grains of sand and grains of seeds, let me explain my thoughts. One grain of sand does nothing. It's almost useless, but combine many grains of sand together with concrete and those grains of sand build empires. It is the same with a seed; one seed offers very little benefit, while many seeds of different varieties feed nations and produce wooden products and life-sustaining vegetation. Think of it. One person can accomplish very little individually, but combine many individual talents together and our accomplishments become unlimited.

My Nonscientific Research of an Alternative Education School

Several years ago, I had the opportunity to volunteer as a tutor and teacher at one of my state's alternative education schools. This school dealt with those youths considered to be at risk. While doing volunteer work at the school, I obtained permission from the school's administrator to conduct nonscientific research of the school to determine if the school was successful in accomplishing its stated goals. This research was not scientific based on a variety of schools. In this research, the students were not our typical high school students. However, they offered an interesting insight into our educational systems and provided thought-provoking questions.

Students who participated in the survey rated the school's programs as highly successful. When responding to the question of what made the school work for them, they specifically cited five areas. The ability to work at their own pace and individual tutoring were cited most often by 35 percent of the students. Freedom to select which subject they gave priority to was cited by 30 percent, and the way discipline was quickly administered was cited by 20 percent, with faculty encouragement 10 percent and personal counseling 5 percent finishing out the categories.

These findings suggest that if at-risk children are given the responsibility and allowed to make choices for themselves, receive tutoring when needed, and are guided by the strict enforcement of rules, they can function well and even learn to respect the system.

Another area of interest was that 100 percent of the students surveyed said that they would not change any of the rules or requirements at the school. This indicated that they respected the strict discipline and high expectations of them. A further example of this was exemplified by 100 percent of the students rating the school as outstanding compared to the public school they had attended.

The three rules employed by the school to govern behavior were cited by the students as being simple easy to understand and follow. These rules were cited by one of the teachers as one of the unique characteristics about the school in that they are easy for students and parents to understand and easy for the school staff to implement.

As a participating observer from January 21, 1997 through April 30, 1997, I believe the most important characteristic about this school that makes it successful is that it's small, and the staff shows a high level of caring for the students. The social worker was always there for the children. He and other members of the staff ate lunch among the children daily, creating a family atmosphere. This was one of the unique characteristics cited by one of the teachers along with the student-staff ratio. My research involved one of the teachers, the social worker, and twenty students from age thirteen through eighteen.

Below are the questions I asked of the students and the responses they offered.

"What is the one thing that has helped you at this school that was not available in the public school you attended?"

Their answers fell into five categories. Freedom of choice and the ability to work at ones pace 35 percent, individual tutoring 30 percent, method of discipline 20 percent, faculty encouragement 10 percent, and personal counseling 5 percent.

"Should programs and methods of instructions like the ones administered at this school be available in public schools?"

Of those asked, 100 percent answered yes. The students stated that they felt the self-paced courses reduced the pressure to perform and helped reduce the feelings of self-doubt and embarrassment among peers. The ability to pace one's self allowed the students the ability to master a particular subject without being forced to move on. They thought that more emphasis should be placed on each individual's ability to learn. They felt that there should be a similar program in public schools for those students experiencing problems adjusting to the public school system.

"Has this school helped you to become a more productive member of your community since attending here?"

Of those asked, 100 percent responded yes, citing improvement in their abilities to communicate with others and in their self-esteem. The Competency-Based High School Diploma Program (CBHSDP) class requiring each student to contact different social agencies within their community to solve problems and gather information helped them to build self-confidence in their abilities to gather needed data to solve personal problems.

"Does having a social worker available at school to counsel you and parents help?"

Of those asked, 100 percent responded yes, stating that they had immediate access when it was needed and that the counselor bridged the gap between parents and students, establishing better communication. Students can tell things to the counselor that they cannot tell to parents, and each student felt that the teachers and staff displayed a genuine concern for them and their welfare.

"Have the four Rs and the three-rule method of discipline used at this school made it easy for you to understand what is required of you? If yes, in what way?"

The four Rs are:

> *Responsibility:* Developing an attitude of having internal control in recognizing clear choices in a situation and accepting the consequences of the choice
>
> *Respectfulness:* Recognizing and accepting the right to decide for one's self and allowing others to decide
>
> *Resourcefulness:* Using existing skills and developing other skills necessary to cope with life in support of one's own life goals and objectives
>
> *Responsiveness:* Showing care for others by listening to and considering their concerns, ideas, and beliefs

This school has three rules to teach the four Rs and address behavior. The first rule is to do nothing that could be dangerous or harmful to oneself, to others, or to property. The second rule is to be in a supervised activity during activity time (from 8:30 AM to 2:30 PM), and the third rule is, when given the "go" signal (call the student's name, pointing to the student and then the door); the student is required to leave the activity immediately and in silence with no gestures. The student may then immediately return to the same activity unless given the "stop" signal (hand held up, palm toward the student), in which case the student must go to another supervised activity.

Of those asked 100 percent responded yes, that the four Rs and three rules helped. The reasons the students cited were the rules are simple and easy to understand, the three rules are easy to remember versus the difficulty in remembering the many public school rules, and the rules are strictly enforced, with immediate consequences for violating the rules.

"What changes at this school would you make that would improve the school to help new incoming students?"

Of those asked, 100 percent answered that they would make no changes.

"How would you rate this school compared to the public school you attended?"

Of those asked, 100 percent rated this school as outstanding. On a scale of one to five, one being poor and five being outstanding, each student rated this school a five.

Below is a list of questions I asked one of the teachers and his response to those questions.

"What are your credentials?"

"I have a doctorate in education."

"How long have you been in this profession?"

"Approximately twenty-five years."

"How many of these years have you worked with alienated or at-risk children?"

"Approximately twenty of those years."

"Have you always been a teacher or counselor/teacher?"

"My career has included many things. I have been a teacher in a regular classroom, special education classrooms, and alternative education classrooms. I have been a counselor in writing programs, special education, and alternative education. I have had a variety of positions as coordinator of programs for special education and alternative education. I have also administered special education and alternative education programs including this program, a program in another city, and I trained teachers in these programs."

"Are there any distinguishing characteristics about the children in programs for alienated or at-risk children that you have noticed over your experiences?"

"Yes, I was involved in some studies at one of the private schools to try to determine what these children's needs are. We used a variety of assessments plus our own experiences working with the children. A large percentage—probably 75–80 percent—would fall into one of the categories that we looked in the area of assessing. Social psychological assessments: what we found in those areas regarding their perceptions of themselves was that they often didn't feel good about their successes or lack of successes in school, so their whole self-concept about school was relatively low. Most of them had stressful kinds of situations that would create almost psychological kinds of concerns; they would have much anger and difficult family problems. Another characteristic we found when they hadn't been successful in school was that they had often fallen two or three grade levels behind academically.

"Another area we assessed was ability. We found that they were not as capable as average students overall, yet they were not in the special education category, so work itself was difficult for them. Using the basic IQ tests, we often found that the things difficult for them were in the verbal area—things that would make them successful in writing, reading, and speaking. We often found them close to average in math—not necessarily *performance,* but ability. Usually children on the average are pretty well balanced in the two areas. In our assessment, we found that children at risk had particular, unique characteristics, such as lack of confidence in themselves, difficulty with school, and situations that created stressful feelings at home or social activity that bothers them from a social psychological perspective."

"How would you evaluate this program compared to others you have worked within?"

"This program has some characteristics that are specifically unique that meet the needs of the alienated or at-risk population. This program has some very clearly defined philosophies that translate into really specific rules and expectations for student behavior that are easy for them to understand, easy for parents to understand, and easy for the staff to carry out. These rules are simple, easy to understand, logical, easy to follow, and make sense to the students. Another characteristic is that it is small, creating a safe environment for them, functioning more as an intact unit and offering student and staff, more support to each other in contrast to a regular school. Another thing that makes it successful is the student-staff ratio."

"Compared to other programs you have been associated with over the past twenty-five years, using the following criteria. The number of students that remain in this program, or enter the competency base program, return to their original school, or receive this school's diploma, how would you rate this program, successful, average, or below average?"

"Looking at all the programs I am aware of—not only the ones I have been involved in—and placing them into categories, you'd have those that are successful, very successful, and those that are not successful. I think this program is not only a successful program, but it is one of the more successful programs. I believe it has become more successful in the past couple of years because it has characteristics I believe to be really important and a part of those other programs that I am aware of or have been involved in that have been successful. They create opportunities for the students to feel that if they invest their time and energy in the program, there is an opportunity for them to leave successfully."

"The thing that's changed in many programs and this one specifically has included other alternatives for graduating successfully—like the competency-based diploma. Programs didn't have this or there weren't very many of them until recently, where schools could offer the adult education besides the regular high school diploma, which is earned via credit. When schools started programs like the competency-based program, it gave students something down the road that they felt they could accomplish. Nothing is more upsetting for us as individuals than being in a situation where we feel we are not going to be successful or there is no chance for us to accomplish anything."

"Often, when kids get into these programs, they feel they are at a dead end. They realize that they are seventeen or eighteen years old and only have four credits and need twenty or twenty-two to graduate. They realize that there is no way they are going to get the credits. Therefore, they think, "Why should I do this work?" If the work relates really well to some end goal they can accomplish, it becomes worth their effort. This program falls into the category of very successful because of the characteristics describe earlier."

"Additionally, it gives students the opportunity to accomplish something and exit successfully so that they can look down the road and know that there is a reason they are studying or doing this. They think, "This is improving my skills, so I can get into the competency-based program, or it's going toward graduation." Because they have an accomplishable program goal, they work to stay in the program. Again, that's one thing that makes this one of the more successful ones I know of."

"Given the authority to initiate something additional to the school that would benefit the existing program, what would it be?"

"I'd create additional components for people initially entering, such as an additional social worker, counselors, additional staff members, tutors, those types of things on the front end."

"We seem to have more students who could benefit from the competency-based component of adult education. Every year, we seem to have more students and can only service about ten students."

"We could service more students if we had a bigger school here. We need additional schools the size of this one. My suggestion is to create more programs like this where students in existing programs now will have a true alternative. If they are not doing well in a regular school, they can select an alternative school like this based on their record in the event that they start falling behind or start having problems with family or the legal system. This would provide a chance for the student to enter earlier—before they have fallen so far behind that they become discouraged."

"From your experience, can a public school operate a similar system, or must it be privately operated?"

"Having been involved in three types of systems—public educational system, private schools, and partnerships—this school in a sense is a partnership, the Department of Education and Child and Family Service. The ones that seem to function more successfully are the partnerships because they allow both agencies as partners to use the resources of two different agencies that may have programs. For example, this school is a unique brand of social service agency which has social workers and counseling components. The Department of Education has the education component, and when the two are placed together, they better meet the needs of the student population we service. Whereas, the public school could administer the same type programs, public school regulations restrict them from doing-so. For example, they are restricted to one counselor per three hundred students; we have one counselor for approximately forty students."

This teacher's experience, remarks, and answers to my questions reaffirmed my belief that our school systems can work better by forming partnerships. The following is my interview with one of the social workers at this school.

"What is your job position title?"

"Social worker."

"Are you trained in dealing with troubled youths?"

"I have my master's degree in general psychology. Through my work and voluntary experiences, I have narrowed my field down to troubled teenagers."

"How long have you been working with alternative schools?"

"Approximately six years."

"Have you noticed any general trends among teenagers in alternative schools versus teenagers in general?"

"Generally, the trend that I have noticed is that there seems to be a breakdown in the nuclear family, whether because of marital problems where the dads and mothers are not getting along or the age-old problem of a generation gap. It seems that the rate kids are growing up is so fast—this includes technology—that for them to hang onto things like traditional values is not satisfactory for their needs. The kids nowadays demand immediate satisfaction to the things they want, so there is no such thing as preparing for the future or saving for the future. They are only interested in what feels good right now. Their outlook is to take care of this need right now, as that's the easiest route for them. Their realms of experiences are drugs, crimes, and sex. That appears to be the general trend to me."

"We have observed through interviews with students that they have a tremendous amount of confidence and trust in you. They have expressed an admiration for your ability to bridge the gap between them and their parents. In your opinion, is this something that can be offered by counselors in public schools?"

"In a practical sense, in public schools, I don't think it would be possible for grade-level counselors to do that. They have so many students to take care of that their types of counseling are bandages in nature—not to solve their problems but fix temporary, as a bandage cover a wound. Ideally, I know counselors are humanistic. They like to help people solve their problems. But I don't think they can in their particular schools at this time, as the work load is too great."

"What's your greatest difficulty in dealing with the students at this school?"

"The best way for me to characterize it is to use the metaphor of an onion. There are so many layers to the types of problems and things they are experiencing at home and outside of school that it appears that the counseling I do—or we do—involves peeling off the top layer of what is going on. There's such a pyramid of things going on that we cannot begin to assist the students with. It's a matter of little victories as opposed to winning the war."

This research is shared with you because it validates my experiences dealing with youths considered to be at risk and youths in general. It seems to me that for the vast majority of our youths who are having difficulties adapting in society, the root cause of their behavior can be traced to factors in their living environment. Many of our children can be saved if someone pays attention to them, listens to them, and offers a kind word of encouragement. While I was volunteering as a tutor and later teacher at the aforementioned school, many of the children would come in and talk to me because I would listen.

The following is a story I would like to share in reference to one of this school's young female students who came in to talk with me one day. She had failed to finish the schoolwork I had assigned her. When asked why she had not completed the assignment, she said, "My parents sent me and my sister out to play with the kids next door."

"Why didn't you explain to your parents that you had a school assignment to complete?"

"They didn't care; they and the neighbors were smoking grass."

"Where were you and the neighbors' kids?"

"In an open lot between our houses and smoking weed, too."

"Where did you and the kids get the weed from?"

"We stole it from our parents."

Fathers, it seems to me that this is one of the worst examples of parenting. If we must participate in behavior of this nature, at home with adolescents growing up is not the appropriate place to do it.

Discovering Myself and My Emotions

In the years of my mid-twenties, a time of self-discovery, I discovered many latent emotions within me—feelings that I had to confront. How could I overcome the feeling that I was inferior, I believe this feeling had lain dormant for years. Incidents would occur involving me and others of different races, and I would often attribute an incident to the fact that I am black. Was this true? Yes, on many occasions, it was, but in the majority of those occasions, I am sure it was not true.

My cultural background had conditioned my mind to think that way. Many of our youths are living in a culture today that fosters unhealthy images. How do we motivate and encourage the child who is hungry tonight? How do we comfort this child who must sleep out in the elements tonight?

As a young child, I was afraid walking those dark roads to my grandmother's house after dark. I cannot even pretend to understand what the child without a house to sleep in tonight feels like. Not only can I not understand what that child feels like, I cannot understand what the malnourished child feels like. I do know what the mental and physical abuse feels like. It made me want to kill. Can you imagine what a child feels like that has no idea who to place blame on or who to reach out to for help?

Many of these children strike out in a negative manner at anyone—more from hurt and frustration than anger. What can we do to assist them in coping with their hurt? Fathers, I believe each of us can assist, if even in minuscule ways. If we pass a homeless child on the streets, we can speak to them in a friendly manner. If the child refuses to speak back, it's okay. They are afraid and nervous, we are strangers, and conditions have not been kind to them.

We can remember the area we have seen the child in and visit that area often. Each time we see the child, we can speak in a friendly manner with a smile. If the child responds, we can be courteous and gentle in our manners; we can offer the child food at one of the eateries. We can ask the child if we can be of further help without being pushy and allowing the child the opportunity to warm up to us. We can check with our local child welfare agencies to see if we can get some professional assistance for the child. Another way we can help at-risk children is to volunteer for programs that work with at-risk youths.

Talk with these children and listen to them; encourage them to trust in their ability to rise above their present circumstances. Share with them the attributes that help you endure. Children need adults to listen to and comfort them; they are social animals with a strong desire to be loved and to feel that they belong. They need to feel a sense of attachment, it the nature of being. If we the fathers or male adults don't reach out to provide a positive image to and for them, we provide them no other choice than to gravitate toward the negative elements of our society.

Many of us who has been associated or worked with youths who are members of a gang have heard these youngsters say that the gangs make them feel as if they belong. Would it not be more beneficial to our community and society in general to make them feel that they are a part of us? How do we do this? We involve them in activities that we are in. We provide outlets for their energy. All teenagers need supervised activity; preferably, they will participate in after-school programs, such as band and athletics.

In situations where there are no such programs or they cannot or will not participate, we the parents must provide that supervision. Many parents I have spoken to have said they don't have the time because they are forced to work from sunup to sunset trying to provide food and shelter. This is commendable that the parents are doing this.

Reflecting back to those days when I worked those farms and the five-acre garden with my father, as well as those odd jobs I did to keep from being around my father after we moved to Savannah. The most important lesson I gained from those experiences was that I was busy doing something constructive, not spending idle time with the guys looking for mischievous things to get into just to feel included.

Many years later, when my sons were teenagers, I owned my own business and was working hard to make a success of it. Spending time with my sons was limited. To compensate for my inability to spend quality time or provide personal supervision, I employed my sons when they were not in school or involved in school activities. I placed each, under the supervision of an adult employee, and paid them, the same hourly rate as the adults.

Attached to their salaries were stipulations; they were to save 50 percent of each paycheck; the other 50 percent was for their use as they saw fit. All other expenses including school expenses were their moms and my responsibilities. They were not always pleased that instead of associating with their friends after school, I had them working. One or maybe both went to their mom and asked, "Why does Pop have us working in our spare time?" My wife spoke to me about their conversation with her. I informed her that she should have sent them to me for the answer; however, I would speak with them.

Later, I had a conversation with the both of them. "Your mom and I both work; we are trying to make life comfortable for you guys. No one is going to give you anything; if you desire something, you must work for it. I am not working you for free or for me. I am paying you the same wages per hour that I'm paying the adults you work with. My only requirement is that you save half of your salary. That you must work is not an option while you are a minor and living in our house."

Did they understand or appreciate this? I don't know. I do know that later they were happy that I enforced that rule. When they became of age to be licensed and drive, each had enough money to buy his first car—paying cash—and this included putting insurance on the car. What I am most proud of is the fact that both became contributing citizens, good fathers to their children, and solid employees. Neither will miss work. They both have said to me, on separate occasions after becoming an adult, "Thank you for giving me, a good work ethic."

Had I not been gainfully occupied growing up, I could have done like many of the guys in my neighborhood have done—either have gone to jail or never have learned the importance of being gainfully employed. Often I see young men my sons grew up with who were allowed to roam the streets after school. Some don't seem to maintain steady employment. One or two have commented to me that when my sons were in school, they did not present the impression that they would be as successful as they have become. I simply smile, thinking to myself, *you would be successful had someone taught you how to work*.

I have discussed children at risk or youths at risk and have offered several opinions on ways to assist these children or youths at risk. In general, this term is used to describe or identify young people who are beset by particular difficulties and disadvantages. It is thought that they are likely to fail to attain the knowledge, skills, or abilities required for a successful and fulfilling adult life.

Why do children become at risk? There are several reasons; I'll name a few, such as family conflict, health issues, homelessness, alcohol and drug abuse, violence, sexual abuse, and financial problems. I believe these are problems that cities and communities must tackle. I would also suggest acquiring the services of someone with good managerial skills to assist—someone who understands the application of key concepts, skills, and best practices of changing organizational behavior in order to help youths at risk.

We need to create change within these high-risk neighborhoods, and one effective way to create change is by using organizational development techniques. The techniques used to implement organizational changes can be effectively applied to change at-risk youths' behavior. Success can be achieved by applying behavior science principles, as well as methods and theories adopted from the fields of psychology, sociology, education, and management.

Organizational change strategies can be effectively applied to these communities with high at-risk youth behavior by establishing a sense of urgency, creating a guiding coalition, developing a vision and strategy, communicating the change vision, empowering broad-based action, creating and building short-term wins, capitalizing on gains, and producing more positive change, thereby anchoring new approaches solidly in the culture. The objective of changing the behavior of at-risk youth is to instill a deep and long-lasting improvement of behavior.

Working toward this objective requires instilling within these communities a sense of urgency about addressing the causal factors contributing to self-destructive behavior. The basis for intervention is rooted in humanistic psychology, promoting cooperation over conflict, emphasizing self-control over institutional control, and providing for participative rather than autocratic management. Changing unacceptable behavior requires a broad coalition of participants, parents, teachers, ministers, political leaders, social workers, and business leaders, as well as members of these communities.

Social psychologist Kurt Lewin developed a three-stage change model of planned change, which explains how to initiate, manage, and stabilize the change process. The first stage, called *unfreezing,* is where the focus is to motivate change, encouraging youth to change old behaviors and attitudes to those desired by society. It's important that parents and community leaders assist by helping to discourage present behaviors and attitudes.

In the second stage, *changing,* incremental changes are undertaken to improve attitudes or behavior. Changing attitudes or behaviors involves learning and doing things differently; and it requires involvement from community members, parents, and the at-risk youth. The final stage, *refreezing,* involves integrating changed behavior and attitudes into everyday life. Once behavioral changes are exhibited, methods of positive reinforcement must be employed.

It's my belief that we can improve positive behavior by cultivating intrinsic motivation. Intrinsic motivation instills a sense of meaningfulness, a sense of choice, a sense of competence, and a sense of progress.

The application of key concepts, skills, and best practices of organizational behavior to helping at-risk youth is beneficial to local communities and to the nation by helping to reduce the crime rate, increasing the quality of education, improving family relationships, improving the quality of the nation's workforce, reducing the homeless population, offering challenges and motivation for youth to be productive members of their communities, and helping to reduce the economic burden on society by reducing the dependence on the social system. In my opinion, applying the above techniques and methods not only helps the child but also communities and society in general.

As I said at the start, there are many conditions within our nation that give me concern. I am expressing one man's experiences and thoughts; there is nothing special about me. I'm a common man who feels the need to speak out and encourage other common men to speak out. I think it's time for us to be heard; there are millions of men and women working hard in the trenches of our communities to make this a better country, and they need much more help. To the millions of you, I call on you to raise your voices. It's time that we are heard.

After Returning from Germany

My assignment in Germany was educational and enjoyable. The Civil Rights Movement within the United States had gained strength tremendously. The Civil Rights Act of 1964 and the Voting Rights Act of 1965 both passed Congress and became law. There was still much racial discord in my native home of Georgia, as well as throughout the southern states. I returned to the United States in January of 1966 and was assigned to Fort Lewis, Washington, to await assignment to a class at the United States Army's Rotary Wing Aviation School.

Once I had my class assignment, I reported to the U.S. army primary helicopter training center at Fort Wolters, Texas, the closest town to Fort Wolters, Texas, is Mineral Wells, located west of Dallas. On entering flight school, I discovered the training to be very demanding, especially the preflight phase. This was an intense month of physical and academic training, as well as constant harassment. Several of the flight candidates were eliminated during the first month.

During the month of preflight training, I gained tremendous confidence in my ability to learn academically. I knew before arriving at the school that I could compete physically; it was good that I could because we ran every place we went for the five months of basic flight training. The academic training was demanding, but I discovered that I had the ability to comprehend the material and learn quickly. My ability was not as deficient as I had thought it to be.

After the first two months, we were allowed a pass from noon on Saturday until 6:00 PM on Sunday, provided we maintained the academic grade requirement. Beginning with the second month of flight training, we would go to classes in the morning and flight training in the afternoon—or flight training in the morning and classes in the afternoon. I still remember distinctly the day I soloed. From the moment my instructor pilot and I entered the aircraft, an (OH-23) helicopter, he was reprimanding me. It seemed that I could do nothing correct, we finally went to the airfield and landed on one of the runways. He said, "I've got to get out and check this sound I hear," getting out of the aircraft and closing the door behind him. He then looked at me and gave a thumbs-up sign. I looked at him and then looked over toward the control tower. It had on the red light for all other aircraft to remain clear of the airfield.

Someone in the control tower called the tail number of my aircraft and said, "You are cleared to takeoff." Suddenly, I had many emotions; I realized that I was cleared to solo. The requirement was to successfully traverse the airfield three times, coming to a complete stop, hovering three feet above the ground, and make a ninety-degree turn towards the control tower on each pass. This didn't take a great amount of time, but to me, it seemed like forever. Try to envision attempting to recall everything you've been taught about a subject instantly—you'll know what was going through my mind.

After completing my third trip around the airfield and receiving clearance to hover to the parking area, the immediate release of tension felt great. When I entered the flight room, my flight instructor met me with congratulatory remarks for an outstanding flight. My fellow students began congratulating me for being the first of the group to solo. The magnitude of this accomplishment began to register on me.

This was in February. There was a tradition that every person to solo would be thrown into the swimming pool at the Holiday Inn. I didn't think they would throw me in on that day because the temperature was in the low thirties. We had a civilian bus driver, and on our way from the airfield to the base, he went by the Holiday Inn—and into that freezing water they threw me. This was a proud, satisfying event and day within my life. At that time, I didn't reflect back, I lived in the moment, and believe me, it was a tremendous feeling.

Years later, as I recall experiences of my life that was a major accomplishment, for a child born to sharecropper parents, abused, and often told, he was not worth the salt in the bread he ate, or the gunpowder it would take to kill him, also repeatedly told he would be in jail before his sixteenth birthday. Those negative comments stirred me to seek what were my motivators.

Surprisingly, my most dominant motivator was my father. His negative comments instilled within my mind that I could not allow him or anybody to think for me. His actions were negative, but they were a positive motivator for me. We all have the choice to turn many negative situations into positive situations. Believe in yourself! You can.

As I look back, my second most important motivator was the young man spoken of earlier—the young veteran that had returned from the Korean War, encouraging me and other young boys to stay in school and graduate. He had recommended that, if after graduating we could not find employment, we consider joining the army. He took the time to talk to and with us. How many other lives he affected I don't know, but I'm thankful that he came into my life. As I said earlier, I don't know his given name. However, I do know his nickname and family name.

After primary flight training, I was sent to advance flight training at Fort Rucker, Alabama. From there, I was deployed to South Vietnam. After returning from South Vietnam, I decided to separate from the military. While serving in South Vietnam in the Mekong Delta area with the Mobile Riverine Forces, my unit's Vietnamese interpreter and I had a very enlightening conversation one day as we stood on the pontoon of the ship my unit lived aboard.

Our conversation involved, among other things, the United States Army's role in South Vietnam. I mentioned the standard indoctrination; we were there to help the South Vietnamese people to live free from Communist domination. This young man looked me in the eyes and said, "That's not true. You are here because the United States wants to be here. We the people of South Vietnam don't care who wins this war. We want the fighting to stop! It's our people who are dying for an idea."

This young man had attended school at one of our nation's top colleges (Massachusetts Institute of Technology). Comprehending his statement was difficult for me, I asked, did he and others really think that way. He repeated it again with emphasis. His comments weighted heavily on my mind. My thoughts was if he—one of their nation's brightest young men—and others didn't care about our being there, then why should I be separated from my wife and two children? Not only was I separated from my family, but also I could have lost my life any day as many had done.

Our conversation came about a few days after I counseled one of my soldiers about a letter he had received from his sister. This soldier had gotten injured a couple of months before for the second time. His sister wrote him, telling him to stop sending mail or allowing the army to send mail to their mother's house. She wrote this letter because their mother was ill. He came to me and gave me the letter to read. After reading it, I inquired as to how I could help. My interpretation of her message was, she opposed the War and used her mother's illness, as a weapon against her brother. All he needed was for someone to confide in; therefore, I listened, as he relieved his emotions.

After comprehending the interpreter statement, I made the decision, if I lived to return to the United States, and rejoin my family I would take my discharge. It was difficult to rationalize fighting a War for a nation, whose best-educated sons didn't want to fight. After arriving back in country, I took my discharge and returned to Savannah, Georgia, to rejoin my family.

My Return to Savannah after Vietnam and the Education of Economically Depressed Communities

On my return to Savannah, I commenced my search for employment. I eventually found employment at Great Dane trailer manufacturing company. The pay was not enough for a family of four to live on, or I should say enough for my family to live the way I wanted. I found another job working for an insurance company as an insurance agent. After a period of training, I was assigned to an all-black, high-poverty area and instructed to use their techniques to sell life insurance policies.

The technique didn't work well for a black selling to blacks. Although I was somewhat successful, their emphasis was on sales and more sales. When my sales were not what the district manager thought they could be, he would often say, "You were not making the amount of money in the army as you are with our company."

His method of sales pressure continued for about a year. During that year, a young man that I had helped to enter the army returned to Savannah in charge of the recruiting station. He often visited me, trying to persuade me to reenter the army. One Saturday morning, this manager decided that he would address me in a demeaning manner in front of the entire sales force, talking about how much I was making with his firm compared with what I was making in the army.

If it was his intent to motivate me with his demeaning behavior, it had the opposite effect. Instead of motivating me to sell more life insurance, it motivated me to reassess my decision to leave the military. About a week after this incident, my friend visited me again. He told me that he had talked with the Department of the Army, and they would allow me to return with the rank I held prior to going to flight school, or I could go back through advanced flight training. I reentered the army with the rank I held before going to flight school and was stationed in the state that would become my home state.

During my brief separation from the military, I lived and worked among people of poverty. I had the opportunity to really see and understand the effects of poverty from an adult perspective. Poverty as defined by *Webster's* implies a lack of resources for reasonably comfortable living. People living in poverty are nowhere near living reasonably comfortably.

Poverty is a condition that affects too many of our citizens. Not only does it affect those living under those conditions, but it affects the wealthy and middle class, as well. Everyone is aware that poverty exists, but how do we eliminate poverty from our society? And what am I doing to help eradicate it? Most of us will probably agree that there will always be segments of society that will remain in poverty, but we can eliminate the vast majority.

To eliminate any condition, one must not only admit that it exists, but also admit that it is an unhealthy condition. For example, if one went to a doctor and was diagnosed with cancer, he or she would want to do everything possible to cure the disease and would commence treatment immediately. One realizes that without treatment, the cancer would spread and eventually destroy the body. In my opinion, poverty is a cancer against society, and it's beginning to eat away at every one of our nation's institutions.

Again, how do we eradicate it? There is no one medication that will eradicate cancer; there is no one remedy to eradicate poverty. As there are many contributing factors to one getting cancer, there are also many contributing factors to one living in impoverished conditions. With cancer, the physician uses many different treatments depending on the type of cancer. Likewise, this same action should be taken with poverty.

Every effort is made to diagnose a disease at its earliest stage. To me, this should be our approach with poverty. Our first effort to eliminate this misery should start with our children. This condition will require all of our efforts—government, private industry, and the public sector. Every child at age three should be required to attend preschool. Several studies have concluded that inadequate education, or lack of education, contributes to poverty conditions.

Proper education begins with the early years of preschool and continues into kindergarten and through twelfth grade. Prior to starting kindergarten, children form their basic thinking skills. Those that do not learn these skills at home start their cycle of education far behind those that do. The majority of children living in poverty do not achieve these skills as do children of middle-class families. Some studies indicate that children living under the conditions of poverty enter school as much as a year and a half behind the language ability of their middle-class peers. It should be mandatory that every three-year-old child be entered into a preschool program.

Many will argue that the state cannot afford the cost of starting such a program and that they do not have the resources to implement such a plan. There is another argument to be made for finding the resources to implement such a program. Think about the following. According to data taken from the U. S. Bureau of justice statistics, the average annual operating cost per State inmate in 2001 was $22,650.00 or $62.05 per day.

Among facilities operated by the Federal Bureau of Prisons, it was $22,632.00 per inmate, or $62.01 per day.
Stephens, James J. (2001), U.S. Department of Justice.

In addition, my state reported it cost $30,870,089.07, to house inmates out of my state for the fiscal year 2003-2004. Hawaii Department of Public Safety, (2007) Annual Report.

These funds have and are being made available to incarcerate an individual. Worst yet, this amount is approximately the amount established as the poverty level for a family of four. The preponderance of evidence indicates that the earlier a child is introduced into a formal educational environment, the greater the probability of success in life. Statistics of parents with a high school or higher education validate the importance of education. Their children seem to adapt and interact better on entering kindergarten than children of parents that failed to finish high school.

It is also a fact that the majority of prison inmates are high school dropouts, and once they have entered the prison system, a majority will return to the system on one or more occasions. Many of these inmates have families that become a cost to the citizens of the state. Several of their offspring will follow them into the criminal justice system. One of the primary reasons their children follow this cycle of behavior is a lack of parental supervision or control. With one of the parents in prison and the other parent working trying to provide for the child or children, this often leaves the child to fend for itself.

Such a proposal can be funded in several ways. First, a partnership should be formed between private industries, local governments, and the individual, with each contributing equally. For example, large companies employing five hundred or more employees could assist by providing on-site space for employees' children that are between the ages of three and four. Local governments could offer tax incentives to encourage large companies to provide the space, and employees with children in this age group could be charged a fee. The fee could be based on the cost of hiring individuals with preschool teaching credentials to teach the children, as well as the cost of providing aides to assist.

Smaller companies in the same geographical location can pool their resources to provide a center, with the local governments allowing them to write off the cost of providing the facility and their employees paying the cost for the educators and assistants. An arrangement of this sort would be beneficial to everyone concerned. The employer creates loyal employees, local governments help to establish a more literate society, and the employees will have their children close to the vicinity of their employment.

Instead of paying for child care, the parents will be paying to ensure that their child has an equal start to a good education. Many of these children's parents are working for minimum wages. By the time they provide food and shelter, they can barely afford to pay for adequate child care. A program of this type or similar in nature would be a win-win situation for everyone.

Another area that needs serious attention is adequate employment at a livable wage. The median income for a family living in my state was estimated to be $67,750.00. This equals approximately $32.57 an hour, or $5,645.83 per month. The local newspaper reported that the median price of a single family home on the Island where I live was $649,000 in July 2007. Gomes, Andrew (2007) Honolulu Advertiser staff writer. With a twenty percent down payment, at an interest rate of six percent this equals a sizable monthly mortgage.

If we scrutinize the employment market closely, we will find very few jobs in any industry that pay above $30.00 an hour. This does not include taxes, utilities, insurance, automobile-related costs, food, medical costs, clothing, or the cost of educating our children. Many of the citizens in our state and nation have reached the critical point of living as many citizens of undeveloped nations do.

Have we in a country of plenty become a nation of dual classes, either rich or poor? We are becoming a nation that relies on third-world nations for cheap labor and material to create billionaires while many of our citizens are homeless and without the basic necessities to sustain a livable lifestyle?

It saddens the heart when one examines the ghetto of many large cities in the United States. In many of the public facilities, such as parks, beaches, underneath overpasses of the freeways, highways, and bus stop shelters, we see the destitute citizens of our country. Many of these citizens are mentally and physically impaired, living on the streets without nutritious food or adequate facilities to provide for personal hygienic needs.

Far too often, when speaking of our military service members, I have heard those who have been injured or killed in combat described as heroes. We say that those who lost their lives made the ultimate sacrifice, and these utterances are true. As a nation, what is our sacrifice? Many of our service members did not lose their lives, but were mentally or physically impaired for life. Are they not heroes, too?

Many of them are the people we see in these ghettos living on the streets and suffering the indignities of a subhuman existence. Worst yet, many of these service members have debilitating injuries and must depend entirely on family or the assistance of a government that asked them to protect our democratic way of life. Do these men and women not deserve better than a meager existence? Should they be forced to beg to survive?

Another issue that's problematic for me is that, for the first time in my lifespan, I do not see future generations progressing beyond the level of their ancestors. Growing up as the descendant of five documented generations of poor sharecroppers, there was hope that I would be able to educate my children, purchase a house, make a home, and save for a comfortable retirement.

This hope for future generations is quickly disappearing. Manufacturing jobs and employment with a good retirement system in this country are disappearing at an alarming rate. Not only is good-paying employment disappearing at an alarming rate, the cost of trying to educate our young people is escalating at an alarming rate, especially at the college level. I seriously believe that we can and that we must do better than we are doing.

Living and working in an impoverished environment after my discharge from the army provided an opportunity for me to join a fraternal organization. Members of this organization were enthusiastically assisting the citizens within those impoverished neighborhoods. I began to see that many good Americans are deeply concerned about those who are impoverished.

They spend many man-hours and dollars attempting to make life livable for some. However, before I speak on the tremendous contributions these men and women make, let me address behavior that I saw exhibited and tolerated within these communities—behavior that is not beneficial to the citizens of impoverished communities. This is an analysis made from living and working amid this group. Again, this is one black American's experience.

There are far too many people that seem to think that the world owes them something for being born. There are far too many that are preying on the weakest members of these communities. There are far too many that have no consideration for our laws. There are far too many that don't value human life. It appears that some destroy life for the pleasure of it. I have seen far too many young men prostitute our most precious gifts—our daughters. I have seen far too many of our young men abuse our women. I have seen far too many of our young fathers abandon their child and that child's mother. I have seen far too many steal others' goods with glee.

Many residents of these communities abhor conduct of this nature. To you the residents of these communities, take action, speak out, and call the authorities when you see unlawful conduct. Remaining silent and choosing not to become involved only fortifies this negative behavior.

The rules of the community reflect the standards by which one lives, as well as the character within that community. It is in the same way that our society's norms reflect the character of our nation. We must notify those that violate our laws that it will cost them dearly. It is the people in this category that need our attention, as well as our young, at-risk population. However, we must change our methods of assisting some of them. By this I mean that if the person is having trouble following our rules voluntarily, we must force him or her to obey, even if it means confinement.

Perhaps it's time serious thought be given to revising our procedures of confining a person to imprisonment. Why should someone who commits a nonviolent crime be confined? Would it not be better to have a system to penalize them financially, even if it's for a period of years? If confinement is necessary for nonviolent offenders, why not consider confinement only at nights and on weekends?

Imaginative methods must be employed to deal with this population. We are paying dearly for this small population. We are paying to house and feed them. We are paying their medical expenses, and if they are married, many of their dependents are on one or more of our social programs. Nonviolent people should be allowed to continue to work if they are employed. If they are not employed, the governing authorities should assist in finding employment for them.

From this employment, they can provide for their families and pay the penalty for their crimes. Many will question whether this is a violation of their rights. I think that they gave up certain rights when they were convicted of a crime against us. If the above violates their rights, maybe it's about time that we reintroduce the dreadful, hated term *chain gang* into many of our prison systems. These people need to contribute to their well-being. We the taxpayers cannot continue to afford the burden of them and their families' upkeep. My question is, can you and I, the middle-class, hardworking citizens, continue to support these people?

The wealthy and elite populations do not feel our burden; they pass this cost down to you and me, either through taxes or increase in materials and food. When the cost of housing and social programs begins to cut into their profits, not only do the above occur, but in many cases, our employment disappears also. Many are then forced into some of the social programs, enlarging the burden on you and me.

We must be creative when dealing with this population. Generations have grown up in an environment that encourages deviant behavior. There is much ignorance among this population; many have endured much to survive and have become insensitive. We have the obligation to force their sensitivity to the norms of our communities through our justice system.

Many of the young men of these communities thrive on corrupting the youth of these communities. It's the "cool" thing to do. These men must be controlled if they refuse to live by community norms. In these communities, several young men walk around with weapons daily. Many give no thought to killing each other. The "black-on-black" crimes in many of our communities are incomprehensible to me.

Our Justice System?

Having grown up, lived and worked among these impoverished neighborhoods and having observed our justice system has caused me great concern. The first element of our justice system is our local law enforcement officials. I have seen law enforcement officials needlessly harass young men of these communities, as if attempting to provoke them into reacting in a negative manner. I've seen police officers intentionally slamming young men up against their patrol cars and treating them in an abusive manner. Conduct of this nature regularly occurs in most impoverished communities, regardless of which large city in whatever state.

Black Americans, many of the problems discussed within these writings are from my experiences—experiences that I am proud of. Therefore, if I address an issue that is disagreeable, it's not done out of maliciousness; it's out of a concern and love for the best of our culture and this nation. I ask that we speak out and become much more involved within our communities. We all share the good things as well as the appalling things.

Let's take a closer look at our justice system. The police are usually the first people the average citizen becomes involved with in our justice system. Since my earliest recollection, I've been told that our justice system is an equal justice system.

We say that justice is blind. If this is true, why are there a disproportionately high number of people of color incarceration in much greater numbers than their percentage of society for identical crimes committed? I could give statistics to support my argument, but one can find all the statistics concerning the population of our penal institutions on the Internet or in a public library.

If we simply look at the statistics, we overlook the issue. By simply looking at statistics, it would be logical to assume that black Americans commit more crime than other cultures. Again, if we study the statistics, it's not true; often, blacks commit fewer crimes in many categories. When brought before our justice system, the penalty is much harsher than it is for the majority race. Why is this? Is it because minority races are not as important to society?

Many questions need to be asked by many of our citizens. How can a system that advocates equal justice under the law administer such unequal justice for identical offenses? We are told that we have the best justice system in the world; with this statement, I agree. There is no nation as just as the United States of America. We are more humanistic than any country I know of, and I sincerely believe in our system of government and our laws.

However, I would like to see that our laws are applied equally and justly. Unjust laws have cost my culture and our nation dearly. Isn't it time more of us speak out on issues that are affecting every American? Many whites believe that what happens to blacks and other minorities doesn't impact the white community. This belief is based on a false premise. The consequences of unequal justice affect the children, the family structure, the social structure, and every working, taxpaying citizen. Having lived and worked in these communities, I've seen the devastating effects on family members.

Many blacks and minority youth are growing up distrustful of their justice officials. This distrust prohibits them from openly communicating with the system. Crimes are being committed that are going unsolved in our neighborhoods daily because many of our young people refuse to assist a system that they feel is unjust to their culture. This behavior is inappropriate, and I think most people will agree that it is inappropriate.

However, this attitude of not wanting to become involved is embedded within socially depressed neighborhoods. Personal observations and experiences with social institutions within these areas have verified the harmful effects for me. Walk into the majority of churches within a black, economically depressed community on any Sunday and listen to the members as they mingle in groups to socialize after services. Eventually, the topic of police brutality or the unfair punishment issued by our courts to a resident of their community becomes the subject of discussion.

Please don't read the above as an implication that it's the subject of all black churches. My analysis for the above statement comes from visiting those economically depressed community churches. In middle-class neighborhoods, a variety of topics are discussed without mention of the law. Over the years, I have seen the same behavior displayed among all cultures and races. This is not a race issue. It's a poverty issue, and it is a behavioral issue. It should not be a justice issue.

What happened to our lawyers? Are they not responsible for seeking equal justice for all under our laws? Did not many go to our nation's most prestigious law schools to study our laws and the practical application of those laws? Is it not inappropriate behavior when a small minority group of lawyers fails to seek the equal application of justice? We have judges cloaked in their robes, the symbolism of equal justice, who dispense this unequal justice, and in many cases, it appears to be dispensed with malice. We, the average American citizens, are paying such a high price for bias in a system that does not represent all equally.

Earlier I stated that I would address a segment of our population I know very little about—our men within the prison population. Before I address these men, please allow me to recall a little history of our justice system as I have learned it. From the earliest period of black American history in our nation, the criminal justice system has been used to ensure that blacks were treated unequally.

During the period of slavery, blacks were rigidly controlled by criminal codes. These codes regulated where we lived, how and where we worked, what god we worshipped, to whom or whether we married, with whom we had children, and whether we raised our children.

The Civil Rights Act of 1866 and ratification of the Thirteenth Amendment was supposed to correct many of those injustices by declaring blacks to be citizens with the same rights enjoyed by the white population. However, immediately following the Civil War, many southern states passed black Codes—laws intended to control a potentially volatile free black population. Those black Codes excluded black Americans from many occupations and denied them the right to vote.

Within the legal system, the conviction rate was much higher for blacks than for whites in the Jim Crow era of the late nineteenth century. At the beginning of the twentieth century, large numbers of black Americans began migrating to the industrial cities of the North. On arrival, many found municipal segregation zoning awaiting them, as well as restrictive covenants by which property owners agreed not to sell to black Americans.

Black Americans lived in communities that were over 90 percent black. The criminal justice system proved to be hostile in those segregated environments. Blacks often complained that police allowed crime to flourish in black neighborhoods and practiced repressive enforcement of minor violations by blacks. Much of the following information cited is taken from

Human Rights Watch and Department of Justice, Bureau of Justice Statistics.

By the 1930s, the arrest rate for blacks was three times that of whites. Black Americans constituted 26 percent of the nation's prison population. It was in the 1930s that the United States Supreme Court began to require the states to conduct fair criminal proceedings. In 1935, the Supreme Court held that the systematic exclusion of all black citizens from jury rolls violated the Equal Protection Clause of the Fourteenth Amendment.

Such changes were only incremental. However, in the 1950s and 1960s, the Civil Rights Movement began to turn many of the southern states' reliance on an oppressive criminal justice system against them. Blacks began a civil disobedience protest, filling local jails. By their willingness to go to jail—and in many instances their insistence on going to jail—with the aim of overwhelming the local courts, they demonstrated to outside observers the injustice of laws of segregation. These acts of civil disobedience helped to bring about the Voting Rights Act of 1965.

Between 1950 and 1980, despite the gains of the Civil Rights Movement, several factors contributed to putting proportionately more black Americans than other races in prisons and keeping them there longer. Those factors included not only higher rates of crime among blacks, but also more aggressive police arrests in black neighborhoods. This also included inequities for poor defendants in pretrial negotiations, higher imprisonment rate for blacks than for whites convicted of comparable crimes, and a greater reluctance of parole boards to grant parole to black prisoners. By 1978, nearly one out of every ten blacks in America had been arrested—three times the rate of others.

By the mid-1990s, the black American incarceration rate reached epidemic proportions. In 1996, 46 percent of our nation's prison population was black. By 1997, nearly one out of every eight black men was in jail, prison, on probation, or on parole. This high percentage of blacks with arrest and conviction records means that large segments of the black population are becoming second-class citizens.

In states where ex-convicts are denied the right to vote, the voting rights of blacks has been eroded. According to a 2000 study by Human Rights Watch, black Americans comprised 62 percent of the drug offenders admitted to state prisons. Nationwide, black men were sent to state prison on drug charges at thirteen times the rate of white men. According to studies conducted by the U.S. Commission on Civil Rights, black Americans constituted 15 percent of the nation's drug users, but comprised about one-third of all those arrested on drug charges and 57 percent of those convicted on drug charges.

Reading and analyzing the above paragraphs should cause one to pause and question the fairness of a justice system that confines one culture to prison at such a disproportionately high rate as compared to the nation's entire population. There was another disturbing set of statistics released in 2002 by the Justice Policy Institute to which all Americans need to give serious thought. It stated that about 10.4 percent of the entire black male population in the United States between the ages of twenty-five and twenty-nine was incarcerated.

This percentage far exceeds other ethnic groups. By comparison, 2.4 percent of Hispanic men and 1.2 percent of white men in that same age group were incarcerated. The number of black men imprisoned had grown to five times the rate it was twenty years earlier; more black American men were in jail than in college. Consider these numbers: in 2000, there were 761,600 black men in prison and 603,032 enrolled in college. In 1980, there were 143,000 black men in prison and 463,700 enrolled in college.

Black Americans are not the only ethnic group that is filling our prison system. Accordingly to the Justice Department's data released in July 2003, the U.S. prison population surpassed two million (2,166,260) people incarcerated in prisons or jails. The report did not count juvenile offenders, but noted that there were more than 10,000 inmates under the age of eighteen held in adult prisons. There was also a noticeable increase in the number of females incarcerated in federal and state prisons; their population was 97,491.

As stated earlier, the prison population is an issue that needs studying. The disproportionately high rate at which Black Americans are incarcerated is an issue that needs intense public scrutiny and discussion. Beyond the scrutiny and discussion of this issue, for the welfare of this ethnic group and our nation, adequate solutions must be found.

As I share my experiences and lessons learned, my motivation for sharing will always be in the hope that something said will better someone's condition. As I read statistics as quoted in the previous few paragraphs, they sadden me. Although I have never been in jail or prison, many of the conditions I have been exposed to gave me an insightful perspective on many of these men's outlooks on life.

I have shared a few of my childhood experiences and my despicable thoughts of killing my father because of his abusiveness to me. I have talked about growing up on a farm, plowing fields with a mule, and many other of my experiences, such as being in the military and living and working in economically depressed, segregated neighborhoods. Now I wish to attempt to paint a vivid picture of what life was and is still like for many trying to escape conditions experienced in these depressed communities.

An Attempt to Paint a Vivid Picture of Life in Economically Depressed Communities

Much of my knowledge come from personal experiences, having lived, worked, and often returned to communities without basic community infrastructure, such as paved streets, pedestrian sidewalks, crosswalks, or streetlights. Many of these communities are heavily populated with minor children and no safe playground for them. My experience amongst all ethnic groups that reside in economic depressed communities is they display similar behavior, towards those not living under the same conditions.

The majority of the black ethnic population commenced its journey within the United States of America as slaves under very appalling conditions. Many other ethnic groups commenced their journey under adverse conditions, too, but they were free and accepted as human beings. As a culture, the black ethnic group has contributed as equally to the economic well-being of our country as any other ethnic group.

The members of this group were denied the ability to develop the one tool—the mind—that is necessary to function intelligently because they were forbidden to get an education.

From those conditions, this ethnic group has risen to contribute much to this nation in every science. Every other ethnic group has also contributed greatly to this nation. Let's examine another group—the white group.

This group civilized a nation. Many people say that they discovered a nation. But for me, the nation was here; the Native Americans were already here. That's another story; we will go back to the white group. This group landed on the shores of a foreign country with the aspiration of making a better life for themselves. Their intellectual ability, determination, and discipline created the best nation in the world for human rights.

For those that disagree, ask yourselves, how many Americans have you seen or know who have died trying to exit our country? This group, with the help of other groups, built the best, most productive nation in the world in less than four hundred years. Members of this group created one of the world's greatest documents—the Constitution of the United States—the document that had the greatest impact of removing the bounds of slavery.

Every black child in these economically depressed communities has a vague awareness of his or her culture's history within the United States. Sadly, very few other ethnic groups have a vague awareness of blacks' history in the United States. This enslavement and denial of educational development to blacks within the United States is taught in very few of our schools or colleges.

It's communicated to black youths by other blacks living under similar conditions. Although the information is not always correct, it's believable. What makes it credible? It is made credible within these communities by actions directed toward them by people of authority. For example, police officers patrolling the neighborhoods will come across a group of young men grouped together doing their thing and not violating any laws. Often those officers will continue to circle the group, and in many instances, the officers will stop and question them as to what they are doing in a group.

Often the police will order the group to disperse. Why? They were not violating any laws. In many of these young fellows' circumstances, it is their only form of social entertainment. Many of them are unemployed and cannot afford going to the theaters or baseball or football games. Some of these young men are employed, but by the time they have spent for the bare necessities to live, they cannot afford other entertainment. Standing on those street corners, telling jokes, and discussing their few adventures seems harmless to them.

Can you imagine their feelings when law enforcement officials break up a friendly gathering? Often from frustration, one or more of the young men will make a comment to the officers. In several instances, the officers stop, place them up against the patrol car with their weapons drawn, and search them. Now, we have added humiliation to frustration. One or more of the young men may say something and then are arrested for failure to obey a police officer.

Situations of this nature involving groups doing nothing other than trying to socialize have resulted in additional expenses to the families of those in such groups. In many cases—in fact, in most cases—the family does not have the financial means of posting bond for their loved one. This means that the individual must remain in jail until a court can hear his case. The confinement could cost him his job.

What choice do these people have? They could either try to borrow the money or lose their jobs. Who do they borrow this money from? The shylock loan companies—those that prey on these communities with their outrageous interest rates. The vast majority of people living in these economically depressed areas are forced to obtain their loans from shylock organizations. They don't usually earn enough to qualify for the best interest rates. In many instances, the families of these young men cannot obtain the money, and therefore the young man must remain in jail. Now this young man has a criminal record to follow him for the rest of his life.

Incidents such as the above occur in other economically depressed, ethnic neighborhoods. However, these young men do not see or hear of this activity. Often the argument is that this segment of society is responsible for the majority of its ills. Some suggest that they are responsible for all of their problems. There are probably partial truths to this argument. However, there is one activity that seems to take place in these black depressed communities that draws particular attention. It's the number of young black men that have been killed or shot by law enforcement personnel.

Often, it is claimed that these men were reaching for weapons, only to discover after investigation that the police officers had lied. One realizes that there are many complex factors to policing depressed neighborhoods. Race, however, should never be a factor, and one should not automatically assume that the police action was motivated by racism.

Our policemen have an enormously difficult job policing any area. Many of these depressed areas are controlled by gangs and criminal elements of our society. As mentioned earlier, how does one explain the "black-on-black" crimes in many of these communities? In several of these communities, it is a daily occurrence for a black to take another black's life. Blacks kill or inflict injury on blacks more than any other ethnic group in our nation. Why? Sure, there is anger, frustration, disappointment, and hardships within the black economically depressed communities. But why harm someone living under the same conditions that you are? One should not kill unless in self-defense. Yet it's an everyday occurrence in many of our large, economically depressed communities.

Incidents like the above happen; it is life today in our country, and we must deal with it. We must teach our young people different methods of dealing with economic hardships. It was life when I was growing up, and it is life today. I have shared my hurt of personal abuse from my father and my eventual comprehension as possible explanations for my father's behavior. There were humiliating and hurtful behaviors demonstrated by some in those depressed neighborhoods, which was incomprehensible to me. Many blacks, with a light skin complexion displayed attitudes, that blacks of a darker skin completion were inferior to them.

Many blacks moved away from these neighborhoods and improved their economic and educational circumstances. A few of those returning blacks displayed the attitude that we were inferior to them because we were poorer. Others returned for a visit dressed in their finest clothes and driving their shiny, new automobiles. As a child my perception of their status impressed me. I wanted money and fine things also, but no one was teaching me how to go about getting those things. Conduct, such as the above-described hurt me. Many in white society were saying blacks were subhuman, and I was seeing Blacks, saying other blacks were inferior, because of a darker skin complexion and economic conditions.

There were blacks returning to those communities, their numbers were much fewer than the requirements needed in those communities. But they came back, expending tremendous energy encouraging youngsters and trying to make change for the betterment of many lives. For many of our children, when subjected to conduct as described, it creates feelings of humiliation, which often leads to devastating consequences.

Conduct of the same was often displayed toward economically depressed adults. These attitudes also created frustration and discouragement for several of those adults. Many adults and youngsters turned to chemicals to assist in finding temporary relief for their feelings. In my younger years, alcohol appeared to be their cheapest temporary relief. As I grew older, I saw other drugs begin to replace alcohol. If one analyzes why most of the black prison population is in prisons and jails today, they will find that drug offenses are the number one crime committed. The sale, use, and distribution of drugs—as well as crimes committed while under the influence of drugs—accounts for the overwhelming majority of their crimes. Instead of relieving their conditions, they are once again victimized.

These drugs are imported into these economically depressed neighborhoods by outsiders offering a quick reprieve to one's feelings of frustration and despair, knowing the individuals accepting their gifts and cheap fixes will become addicted, which of course provides a source for their illegal revenues.

Please note that I do not attach a specific race or culture when I refer to economically depressed neighborhoods. My knowledge of the predominately black economically depressed communities has been limited the past thirty-five years. I have also lived within comfortable, cosmopolitan communities. What I have learned over the years is that the behavioral traits of others are much the same in economically depressed areas, regardless of race or culture.

Fewer children in these economically depressed communities graduate from high school. More of their young females become pregnant at an earlier age, there are more one-parent homes, and there is much more involvement with law enforcement authorities. If these issues are to be improved upon, it will take more involvement on the "block"—the streets of these depressed communities.

For those of you, who have succeeded in removing yourselves from these communities, please listen to the voices crying for help to get out and do everything possible to help them achieve their goals. To the many who have achieved wealth and power, please consider lobbying our nation's leaders to raise the minimum wage laws to a level that allows families to live above the poverty level. I will address this subject later.

Fathers and men of our prison population, to many of you of this group, I simply don't understand your motivations. I well understand being poor and not having any money. I well understand being perceived as "less than" by others, but I don't understand the psychology of committing offenses against one's fellow man or doing anything that's going to curtail one's freedom of movement or limit one's ability to better his conditions.

When reading or hearing that a young black man has taken the life of another black man, I find myself asking, "Lord, why?" Of course, I don't get any answer. Therefore, I ask myself why, and I consciously think over my experiences among people of economically depressed ethnic groups for my answers. Over the years, I have failed to discover any satisfactory answer for this behavior.

My experience with and knowledge about this population is very limited. The few people I knew who went to prison or jail did not impress me as people to be associated with. Many will probably question my reason for saying this. Please allow me to share my perception of the majority I did meet. They appeared to be self-centered and gave no thought or consideration for the other person or that person's welfare.

I have questions about things that are incomprehensible to me. For example, how can an adult man molest a minor child, male or female? How does one rape a woman? Does this individual not have a mother or sister? How does one sell addictive drugs to our young people in elementary and high schools? How does one physically abuse the woman he has taken to be a part of his life? How does one prostitute and abuse our young women? Many of the crimes some of our prison inmates have committed are incomprehensible to me.

Stealing from a grocery store is understandable if one has a starving family at home and cannot find work and cannot beg or borrow enough money to get them fed. One understands making a mistake. One understands doing something stupid for the fun of it. If one is caught and sent to prison, how can that person not learn and not repeat his actions? Maybe one can empathize with the individual that commits a nonviolent, economic crime or crimes that do not violate our children. One can empathize when no lives were placed in danger, but even empathy stops when one continuously violate our laws. My friends, associates, and I cannot empathize with those who commit hideous crimes, such as murder, attempted murder, rape, and especially rape or molestation of any child. Most of my friends and associates and I will and have forgiven many of you for crimes committed. However, crime like those addressed above requires extensive rehabilitation and retribution before forgiveness can be requested or given.

My personal viewpoint is that if one takes another's life, intentional and willingly, that person should remain in jail for the remaining of his or her life. Obviously, this is my belief for taking of one life. For the willful and intentional taking of more than one life, this individual must never be released from prison—period. I am against the death penalty; my belief is that, unless one can restore a life, one should not take a life. I am old enough to realize that one can commit the crime of taking a life and then deeply regret the decision and atone for that act. This person must and should be forgiven and allowed freedom again.

To some the above statement might be confusing. But to me there is a difference between willful and intentional killing than causing a death. Killing someone in self-defense, by accident, or to protect a family member is not intentional or willingly. Mitigating motives are often contributed to their actions; therefore, we should evaluate and treat them with compassion.

As I have stated earlier, I thought of taking my father's life for my sixteenth birthday. This was the most despicable thought of my entire life. But, living with my father, I gained an insight into one's life by evaluating the whole person—the good and the bad. Both make the person, and when both are analyzed, one gets a clearer understanding of the person.

Another belief of mine is that those convicted of horrendous crimes other than murder and child molestation should be made to work on a chain gang. Many reading this will probably think my ideas are out into left field—and maybe they are—but please think along with me for the next few lines.

Every person is a human being. We must live together, and to live together requires acceptance or rejection of others' thoughts and opinions, but not the person. Our humanity allows us to establish laws to govern the masses based on majority opinion. I know that there are problems with the system. However, one living within the United States of America can be considered blessed, as we have a great system. No one owes anyone anything other than an equal and fair opportunity.

We do not owe convicts food, housing, or recreation. Those habitual law violators should not be allowed to lie around, eat, and sleep while the American taxpayers support them. They must contribute to their upkeep. The American taxpayers are contributing to the welfare of many of their dependents. The vast majority of American citizens provide for their own family and their welfare.

There is a special group of American citizens that has contributed tremendously to this nation, and many have lost their lives. Others are gravely injured for life, and still others have served honorably for years. They are our military personnel. These men and women have given their all, yet we don't provide them free room and board to include medical care. Being a member of the military group was an honor for me. The overwhelming majority of the military population firmly believes in providing for themselves and their families and in protecting our nation and the laws that makes us a free nation. They gladly protect the rights of our prison population. Should we not have the right to expect the prison population to share some responsibility of caring for themselves?

There are other groups that deserve some attention—gangs. These groups have destroyed many lives and communities—

and for what? Selling drugs? Owning territory? Proving their masculinity? Again, I have a lack of personal experience, but judging from data, the journeys of most gang members take them to prison or death. As they travel their journey, they destroy thousands of lives. How long can a society neglect to take complete control of such situations?

These are questions that need a unified discussion. This discussion must include all races, genders, senior citizens, and the prison population. Why the prison population? Because when one listens closely, one discovers a message is delivered by all. Careful listening can provide valuable information. On occasions, negative or adverse sources of information prove to be more valuable than positive sources of information.

We are intelligent people. Look how progressive this nation has been. We must use every effort available to rid our communities of these gangs. As a nation, we attempt to negotiate with other nations before declaring war. These gangs operate in the same way as do nations that operate against our best interest. We should attempt negotiations with the stipulation that we are going to declare war on disruptive and criminal behavior. I suggest negotiation. One might ask: What does he means by negotiation? What do gangs have that society needs?

May I suggest that they have control of too many of our young people through the use of drugs? They also have control of an illegal underground economic system, a system that has placed a tremendous cost on the citizens of our nation. What is my recommended starting point? Our government supplies billions of dollars per year to undeveloped and developing nations in an attempt to persuade them to support the policies we deeply believe in. We do this through negotiation. We have made contributions and offered loans to nations that could not repay them, and we have written these loans off.

Should we not place as much emphasis on economically depressed neighborhoods within our country? We can negotiate with these economically depressed communities. Let's provide grants and economic aid packages to stimulate jobs and industry growth to eliminate much of the unemployment. Of course, these communities must comply with negotiated standards. We could even offer a small stipend to children who maintain a specified grade level. Is this a form of bribery? Yes, of course it is. The object is to change destructive behavior and eliminate the infectious cancer of ignorance and poverty from our society.

And, as another thought, why not consider legalizing marijuana and cocaine, selling it from controlled locations, charging an excise/user tax, and placing this tax into a medical fund to treat the aftereffects later? This suggestion might be unpopular with many citizens, but maybe it is time we have a serious, intelligent discussion instead of an emotional discussion on the subject. Our nation declared war on drugs decades ago. According to broadcasted data, more drugs are entering the nation today than on the date war was declared on drugs. Today, those characters termed as "drug lords" are shipping more drugs into our nation with highly sophisticated equipment. Obviously, they have a good market for their drugs. They have a network of distribution characters peddling these drugs, thereby killing our young people and destroying communities.

Eliminating this cancer from society requires all of our efforts. What good will legalizing a destructive drug do? Maybe it will remove greed, corruption, and destruction by removing the profit. Many will say yes, and then we will be building a nation of addicts. This may be true. But we built a nation of cigarette smokers and alcohol abusers, and through education and controls, we are bringing those two addictions somewhat under control.

The legalization of drugs will not eliminate the trafficking of illegal drugs; of this we can be assured. There is too much money in this illegal trade. Maybe legalization and taxation can eradicate the profitability of the trade. There is another aspect to this issue that should be studied. What is the economic cost to society created by the aftereffects of illegal drugs now? What is the moral cost of illegal drugs to society? How many of our children are we prepared to lose to this cancer on our society?

There appears to be a great demand for marijuana and cocaine within our country. This is apparent by the amount of drugs confiscated by our law enforcement officials yearly. We are paying the medical costs of treating the aftereffects of these drug users today. At least legalization and taxation, with the funds being placed into a health and welfare fund, will assist the taxpayers in paying this expense.

Personally, I have no grounded position on the legalization of drugs. However, I have a grounded position on Americans removing gangs and criminal activity associated with gangs. They are destroying us from within. There will be more to follow later on this element of our society.

My First Arrival in Hawaii

After arriving in Hawaii in March 1970, at my new duty station, the state which would become my state of permanent residence, new opportunities of learning were open to me. I began to intermingle among the various ethnic groups and gained favorable insight about the state's cosmopolitan way of life. Try to imagine the learning opportunities presented to a man born into a segregated society on a Georgia farm.

With every available opportunity presented to me, I discovered three of the major islands of Hawaii. Earlier, I mentioned having the opportunity to join a fraternity while living and working in Georgia before reentering the army. This fraternity had a chapter in Hawaii. I became affiliated with it and became involved with the physically impaired citizens on the island of Oahu. Through this organization, I had the good fortune of meeting three gentlemen who were dedicated to assisting those in need. They provided me with a comprehension of the necessity of assisting those impaired within our communities.

Many events took place in my life while I was assigned in Hawaii. Originally, I was assigned to Schofield Barracks and later transferred to Fort Shafter. It was shortly after arriving in Hawaii that my family joined the statistics of many military families, my wife and I divorced. It was while serving my first tour of military duty in Hawaii that I had the opportunity to meet many of our nation's mayors. The mayors held a convention in Waikiki, and my fraternity held a reception for them. This event provided me with my first opportunity to mingle among politicians, and it was a very impressive occasion for me.

To me, these mayors represented upper-class men who were unapproachable to a majority of the citizens I had been associated with, to the majority of my associates. Those men were respected as honorable, men of character, and represented the best of our nation. The occasion was educational and memorable for me.

One of the three men previously mentioned and his wife were the founders of the Miss Black Teenage Pageant of Hawaii. He also served as the executive director of the pageant. This man was a mentor to me. He had this enthusiastic ability of volunteering for community service.

This man was a retired army major. He had served in World War II and in the Korean War as a military chaplain. This man had a compassion for his fellow man that was admirable. Another gentleman of the fraternity who was inspirational to me was also a World War II veteran. He received a battlefield commission in combat to the rank of captain. After the war ended, he was rifted from captain back to the rank of first sergeant.

This gentleman had no college education while on active duty; he eventually obtained a Master of Science degree in public administration. My chaplain friend graduated from college prior to entering the army; he also had a master's degree. These two men and another World War II Navy Medical Corps veteran who separated from the navy and opened a business in Hawaii taught me the meaning of integrity.

I didn't fully comprehend or appreciate this lesson until many years later. These men demonstrated the very best America has to offer. They were Americans dedicated to the safety of our nation and committed to our people. All three were black, but they were Americans first.

Throughout, I will be talking about black Americans. Many prefer the term "African Americans." I have no objection to the term. However, I personally know very little about Africa, and as far as I've been able to trace my family generations before me—from 1821 until the present—we were born in Bullock or Screven County, Georgia, the United States of America. When I went to Vietnam to fight, I didn't go as an African. I went as an American. Several Americans have had problems trying to identify my nationality. I am American—born, raised, and educated.

These men exhibited the same attitude. Looking back, they probably molded my mind-set. I know with certainty that they had a positive influence on my life. Over decades, attempting to analyze events that shaped my character, I'm certain that positive role models and my environments were major contributors.

As with all career military men, my duty stations changed regularly. In the spring of 1973, I was redeployed to Colorado Springs, Colorado. This deployment placed me back within an armored cavalry unit, my first such assignment since my early days in Germany. In this unit, I was assigned as a platoon sergeant without a platoon leader. This was a challenging assignment.

Many of the men of this platoon were returning veterans of the Vietnam conflict. Several of our nation's citizens were exhibiting disturbing behavior toward those men and me because of their personal dislike of the Vietnam War. Some of these men—including myself—felt they had made great sacrifices for our country, and some of the men felt betrayed, hurt, and disappointed. Others considered military discipline in a peacetime garrison environment as a waste of their time and effort.

My responsibility as I saw it, being a junior leader in the United States Army, was to instill military discipline, which I interpreted as obedience of orders issued by those of superior rank and self-discipline enough to do the things expected without individual supervision. To fulfill this obligation required that I learn and perform the duties of the position in an exemplary manner. I had led men in combat in South Vietnam. However, this assignment was a completely different challenge.

Knowledge I had previously learned—but had not fully appreciated before—was that regardless of the occupation one is engaged in, to lead, one must be willing to seriously consider and evaluate the opinions of others. One must balance the need for open communication with that of the objective or mission while following the orders of those appointed to lead.

If one disagrees with a decision, that person has an obligation and duty to disclose his or her disagreement. If the disagreement is not discussed or considered, it becomes that person's obligation to proceed to the next level of authority. Some of those men needed to be reminded that America is a great nation that cares for all its citizens. Those demonstrating against the war and the military were also good citizens, and they loved their country as we did.

Some needed to be reminded that the greatness of our nation is that one has the ability to express his or her beliefs freely. Several of these soldiers would leave for a weekend pass and extend it into a three-day weekend. Because of my belief in obeying the laws as they are written, I applied pressure to ensure that military rules were strictly complied with.

This assignment taught me one of many valuable lessons. It was my first major leadership role in peacetime; leading men in combat is entirely different—or at least it was for me. In combat, one has a captive audience. One realizes that safety depends on learning, cooperating, and following orders. Learning the techniques of getting others to support my orders and actions willingly was rewarding. This assignment also taught me humility and an understanding of the tremendous sacrifices made by the military families, the incredible support of spouses, and the willingness of service members to forgo spouses and family for the needs of their country.

Was all of this done out of patriotism? No. For many men like me, the military was our best option. Our objective was to take the option and do the best we could with it. Many Americans from the lower economic income level within the United States have seen the benefit of serving this country through the military as a movement up from poverty. Sadly, in my opinion, this option is becoming much more of a burden on those of our nation who least benefit from this nation's wealth—our economically depressed. I've come to realize this over the years.

It was on this assignment that I realized that I was maturing as a man, both physically and mentally. People in general began to take on a different meaning to me. My military superiors placed extreme confidence in my ability to lead a platoon. They refused to place a commissioned officer over the platoon.

Why am I sharing this with you? Because little, simple steps for some are giant steps for others. Nothing is or was exceptional about my experiences. Millions have done and are doing these things today. I have enjoyed my life, but I'll cover this later. It was this assignment that tested my ability to lead. This training proved to be invaluable for me on my subsequent assignment at Fort Wainwright, Alaska.

My Alaska assignment tested my durability as a man, with temperatures reaching fifty-five degrees below zero in winter months. I was the platoon sergeant of one-of-a-kind platoon in Alaska. This platoon consisted of thirty-five men. Every man of the platoon had to be a good cross-country and downhill skier. Leading and training men for combat in these conditions reveals much about a man's ability to cope and survive. Over the remainder of my military career, I had many challenging assignments in several locations.

Many social changes were taking place within the United States. In my opinion, many of those changes were a direct result of the Civil Rights Movement in the 1950s and 1960s. These changes were being reflected in the military in a more visual manner for me and others who had grown up in segregated, economically depressed communities. We began to see upward mobility of minority races. It was no longer an oddity to see black commanders at every level of command, from platoon to division and even commanders at army level.

For black men of my age, this was confirmation that generations of minority groups' dedication, loyalty, and devotion were finally being recognized. Within my mind, the progress minorities were experiencing, even in the military, was as a direct result of the leadership ability of Dr. Martin Luther King Jr. I was aware that millions had worked with Dr. King for this display of equal opportunity, including me. However, in my opinion, Dr. King had inspired a nation to closely examine itself and see the quality of the individual, not the color of one's skin. I will speak of my feeling and thought reference Dr. King later.

I attributed much of the progress I saw to affirmative action programs. Whatever the contributing factors were, these events represented improvement. Many people had different opinions and did not see these developments as positive contributions for our nation. Many displayed the attitude that these minority groups were being rewarded because of their race. I and others considered many who expressed those sentiments to be insecure and ignorant of our environment. These changes were causing many concerns. However, thanks to our military, actions were taken to inform and educate. All military personnel were required to attend racial relations and equal opportunity classes regularly.

My employment experiences definitely favor the military. Our military has all of our society's fallacies amid their ranks, yet they communicate, coordinate, and cooperate as a team of one.

My Rewarding and Valuable Experiences Voluntarily Working with Various Communities

In my last few years before retiring from the army, I became actively involved in voluntary activities within different communities through my fraternity and other civic and social organizations. Working within these communities provided me a valuable and rewarding education. Please allow me to share this educational experience with you. I live in the state of Hawaii, “the Aloha state,” on the island of Oahu. Hawaii is often referred to as paradise, and to me it is.

Hawaii has a multitude of ethnic groups and cultures, and among these groups is cultural preference. For example, three small mixed ethnic groups are at the football stadium tailgating, one group does not know the other. Before long they will be intermingling, and shortly thereafter, the intermingling becomes among those sharing cultural characteristics. This culture preference is healthy as long as it doesn’t affect the minority cultures involved in a negative manner. The people of Hawaii have mastered the technique of integrating the masses to live in peace and harmony with each other, better than any state I have lived or worked in.

After retiring from the army, I went into the building and ground maintenance service business. I also maintained an active participation in civic and social organizations. After a few years in the building and ground maintenance business, I decided that it was not for me. I sought civilian employment for the first time since my discharge from the army in 1968. I applied for employment as a bus operator with the company that operates the public transit system for the City and County of Honolulu and was accepted.

This acceptance was anticipated. I had served several years as the senior enlisted member (first sergeant) of a company-sized unit of approximately 150 members and had years of experience as a battalion operations noncommissioned officer. I was the senior enlisted man responsible for the daily operations, of my battalion's operations and tactical operations center. I had several certificates and letters certifying my demonstrated ability to lead, organize, supervise, train, and manage men.

With the above credentials, I felt positive that I would be hired and allowed to progress among the ranks to one of the supervisory positions within the company by exhibiting a good work ethic. After working there for approximately two years, I realized an opportunity that had not availed itself to me before—the opportunity to attend college full time while being fully employed.

With this employment, I could work the late evening shifts while attending classes full time during the day. I started college at one of the community colleges and obtained an Associate of Arts degree in liberal arts. As a result of my leadership positions within my fraternal organizations, my military experiences, and my exposure to the social sciences classes in community college, I decided to seek a degree in social sciences. I graduated with a Bachelor of Arts degree in social sciences with a specialization in political science and sociology.

Let me share with you the lessons I learned during this period. While driving those city buses late at night, I had the opportunity to meet many members of the commuting public. Many of those passengers would catch my bus in the late afternoon, leaving one place of employment and traveling to another. Many of those same passengers would then catch my bus on my last trip of duty at around midnight on their way home. These passengers varied in age, their commonalities were each, was working two or more jobs.

It often occurred to me that these people had families with small children, and it must have been really tough on them working two full-time jobs to survive. These people were and are nice to be with. They exhibit the best of America's character. If the bus operator was late, they would still greet them with a pleasant greeting. They never complained about the operator being late; they automatically assumed that an accident or road closure had delayed the bus.

This group of men and women were honest, hardworking, family-oriented people trying to hold onto a piece of the American dream—the dream of providing for their families and sending their children to a quality school and the dream of their children having a successful life. Many of the passengers of that group were working two jobs and still barely surviving.

They maintained hope. I am told that hope is the motivator of the human soul. Maybe that is what kept them going in such a friendly spirit. Hawaii like many other states was losing mills and factory jobs. Along with the elimination of the sugar and pineapple industries was the elimination of many common labor jobs. Much of my state's labor market at present depends on tourism.

There are other groups that bus operators come to know well. One of these groups contains many characteristics combined into one. They are our homeless people. As stated earlier, I drove late nights. One of my routes took me about four hours from the time I departed the bus terminal until my arrival back at the terminus. This was the last bus to partially circle the island. Several of my homeless passengers, male and female, had mental disabilities. Those who affected me the most were females with small children. Many would go to the rear of the bus and fall asleep. They would not wake up before we returned to the terminus. Others were drug or alcohol dependent. The people in this group were seldom troublesome but were rather more of a nuisance for the bus operators. Bus operators have a unique opportunity to study human behavior. Each member of the groups I have mentioned exhibited specific patterns of behavior. It was often difficult for me to see some of these people without feeling a sense of empathy for them.

Homeless people are in all major cities. If you are interested in finding a city's underprivileged, ask a bus operator who drive late nights and early mornings. Many of these homeless people are mentally impaired. One does not have to be a psychiatrist to recognize this. Most are harmless; they mumble to themselves ever so often or carry on a conversation with an imaginary person.

One could see the shame and humiliating expression on many of the homeless mothers' faces as they pushed their children toward the rear of the bus. Often I found myself wondering where the children's fathers were. Were these children in school? How were these children eating? I think we are a better nation than we are showing. Some will say, "That is happening in Hawaii." To you, I say, "That is true, but look around your cities."

One of my most rewarding experiences was being a member of one of my fraternities and being elected as its president for my state. I traveled to many states and cities. In each of those states and cities, I saw many underprivileged citizens in parks and sleeping on steam grates on the sidewalks.

Conditions like those described are seen by many citizens of our nation. Many of this nation's citizens are working hard daily and assisting this population of our society. They need additional help from all segments of our society. When I refer to all segments of society, I am referring to the leaders of religious institutions, educational institutions, social organizations, government institutions, communities, and individuals.

We must come together and discuss the deteriorating social conditions of our nation. Discussing the issues will not solve the problems, but it will place them before the public, out in the open. Over the years, I have often questioned my understanding of several of our social institutions. Does not the word "social" refer to establishing an interdependent relationship? Many leaders of our social institutions have abused their positions and authority, as well as using and abusing others to enrich themselves. Behavior of this sort is shameful and especially when displayed by our elected officials.

Operating city buses provides tremendous opportunities for one studying social behavior. It offers the opportunity for one to observe different patterns of behavior among different cultures and different social levels, such as those of professional workers, administrative workers, office workers, nurses, and so on, as opposed to laborers, construction workers, and so on. The observation of vehicle drivers is an entirely different experience, especially when stuck in traffic.

There are some drivers out there who are angry at the world. There are those who eat, shave, apply makeup, and talk on their mobile phones while driving. There are those that resist allowing others to get ahead of them in traffic, and there is a host of other types of attitudes. If one had questioned me in earlier years about driving a city bus, I would have responded, "No, thank you." After closing my business, it was necessary to find employment. My spouse was working, and I had retired from the army years earlier, but I still needed to work. The City and County of Honolulu was hiring bus operators.

This proved to be a very satisfying and rewarding job for me. The most rewarding aspect of working as a bus operator in Hawaii was the multitude of cultures and nationalities I had the privilege of meeting and communicating with. Millions of visitors come to our state yearly to vacation and enjoy our climate. Communicating with these visitors was a rewarding and educational experience for me.

The things the vast majority of these visitors shared in common were the love of their families, their home states, country, and their desire to socialize while attempting to learn as much as possible about the Hawaiian culture. When communicating with these people, one realizes that we are all basically the same. We are proud of our families, communities, and our heritage. Very few of these people speak of the depressing and unsatisfactory conditions within their families or communities. These are issues all of us would prefer to keep under cover, or as my generation would say, "Do not wash your dirty laundry in public."

Washing one's dirty laundry in public is the only way to clean the laundry at times. When the dirty laundry becomes smelly, affecting our neighbors and us washing the laundry must take place in privacy or in public. In many of our communities, our dirty laundry has become a public nuisance, or I should say public disaster? Much of this dirty laundry is our children. Fathers, how can we honestly call ourselves good men and do nothing to assist in cleaning this dirty laundry?

If our child comes into the house muddy and filthy from running and playing outside with other children, would we allow that child to jump on the sofa or lie across the bed without washing and cleaning up first? I really don't think that many of us would. Yet many of us see our child come home with his pants off his waist almost down to his knees without saying anything. I have talked to some men about this craze and have been told that it's a minor thing. The people of the younger generation are expressing themselves. My reply is "You think it's a minor thing? Who do you know that is interested in looking at the crack of someone's behind?"

Fathers, for our children to survive in the era we live in today, they must be taught good judgment and receive a good education. You and I may not be equipped to offer a good education, but the vast majority of us know what the concept of decency is. We understand and know that we cannot go to apply for employment at any firm with our pants down to our knees and expect to get hired. Many would say this is a small issue. Others would say it is an insignificant issue. With those comments, I simply disagree. Allow me to use an example of something I didn't understand growing up to explain the importance of small and insignificant issues.

Remember—I grew up on a farm. The ground around our house was dirt; there was no lawn. When the wild grass began to grow in the yard, my parents had me and my siblings who were old enough to hoe the grass and then rake the yard clean. Every week we would have to rake or sweep the dirt—not because trash was in the yard, but simply to remove tracks to give the appearance of a neat and clean yard. Why was this important?

My parents realized that training us to take care of the minor things would carry over to us taking care of the important things, such as keeping our rooms clean, scrubbing the wooden floors within the house, and washing our clothes in a washtub with a scrubbing board when they became dirty. Minor—but extremely important—chores not only taught the importance of cleanliness, but those chores removed germs and diseases from the house. My parents understood that we were economically depressed, and they could not afford medical coverage. Therefore, we had to keep our surroundings as sanitized as possible.

Many of my observations while living and working within economically depressed neighborhoods concerned me and caused me to reflect upon the possible parenting skills of some in that population. Many of the houses would have trash all over the front porch. The yards would be unkempt. Many of these parents would be working jobs from morning until dusk.

It was easy to understand why they did not have the energy or time to clean the place. What was bewildering to me was that many of these people had teenaged children who would be at home or out into the street playing with other children. Why were these parents not assigning chores to those children? Do we not have an obligation to teach cleanliness and household duties to our youngsters? Do we not teach responsibility, discipline, and work ethics when we assign chores and individual tasks?

These are small, simple things, but they serve a larger purpose. For example, assigning these teenagers the responsibility of cleaning the kitchen and the yard and washing the clothes causes much of their time after school to be occupied. Once they have completed their chores, they should be required to study and produce the material they have studied to their parents after those parents arrive home from work.

The benefit of the child doing chores and schoolwork prior to the parent coming home from work ensures that the child is at home occupying his or her mind in a positive, productive manner. Too many children are running the streets and socializing without adult supervision. Many of the parents I saw could not tell you where their child would be when they arrived home after work. A child should never be allowed to leave home without the parents' permission and knowledge of the general vicinity this child will be visiting.

Parents, this is one man's opinion, but I grew up this way. I raised my children this way, and thanks to my deity, none of my children or grandchildren have been members of a gang or gone to jail, and I haven't, either. Thanks to my deity, none have been killed or injured in unlawful activity. If I give the impression that I am proud of this, you are reading me correctly; I am extremely proud of this fact.

Again, the above is no big accomplishment. The majority of American families have done the same. This is not about us. It is about the minority that is costing our communities and society much pain and destruction. It is not about being economically depressed. It is about attitude. It is about responsibility, and it is about dignity.

These are things that can be changed by leaders of these communities. It takes caring, coordination, and a desire to improve these lives. There are several ways in which this can be accomplished. Please allow me to espouse my thoughts as you read. We can organize church groups, college fraternities, social fraternities, and community groups to sponsor community clean-up day once a quarter or as regularly as is feasible to clean and beautify common community grounds.

In those communities where juveniles have come into contact with the law for minor offenses, I believe it would be beneficial for the leaders of these communities to form coalitions and appeal to the civil authorities to have these youths sentenced to community clean-up details. These youths should be assigned into the area they live in. I even suggest that they be forced to wear outer clothing that reads "I am a community offender."

Many will say that this is degrading and that it would affect the child's self-esteem. This may well be true. From my perspective, it is better to degrade this child and cause a little loss in self-esteem than having this same child eventually hurt someone or commit a serious crime later that requires confinement by society at a cost to many of our innocent and productive citizens.

Many of these youths commit petty crimes throughout their adolescent years. Our civil authorities often smack these kids across the wrist and sent home to parents who are lacking in parenting skills. These same adolescents reappear as adults in our justice system. Not only do they reappear within our criminal justice system, many have parented children and taught them to repeat their cycle of conduct. I do not have the answer to solve all the issues within these economically and socially depressed communities, but I am willing to discuss and work with anyone to change this destructive and deviant behavior.

Fathers, I have spoken of us being teachers to our children. I feel this is a good time for me to address many of our attitudes as I have observed them toward our daughters. As stated earlier, I cannot address our mothers in a comfortable manner because I cannot empathize with their thought patterns, but I feel comfortable addressing issues pertaining to our daughters.

Some of my saddest moments have been seeing our young teenage daughters on the streets prostituting themselves for money. Where are these children's fathers? Not only are many of our daughters prostituting themselves for money, many of them walk out of our houses displaying the manners of prostitutes, whores, or sluts—whatever terminology you choose to use.

Many of these young women and several older women walk out of their houses wearing halter-tops and shorts that do not cover their hips. Many of these women wear G-strings or thongs showing the crack of their behinds. Fathers, many of us see this and allow the child to walk out of our houses in this sluttish manner. Am I prudish? Perhaps so, I don't think so; I love to see beautiful, sexy women. I live in a state with beautiful beaches and plenty of beautiful, sexy women. I enjoy the sights, but I also love classy women. I felt an obligation and duty to inform my daughter when I felt her dress was inappropriate for an occasion.

Fathers, in my experience dealing with the young females, it appeared to me that daughters idolize their fathers. Mine do, and not only do my daughters idolize me, my granddaughters do, too. Am I blessed? Yes. Why do I feel that I am blessed because the young females of my family idolize me?

It is because it's a signal that they recognize that I have treated them with love and respect as a person. It's a sign that they appreciate our talks and my listening to them, as well as allowing them to question my advice. This is normal behavior for the majority of fathers I associate with and most fathers in America. If you do not believe this, look around us. We have young women who are exceptionally intelligent, articulated, and successful in every profession and science there is.

It is the daughters that are being abused, sexually molested, and degraded that I hurt for. In this book, I have said that I hurt on several occasions. Believe me, I really feel heartache and sadness for these children. I know, with concerted efforts, we can change the behavior that contributes to their conditions. But first we must look to ourselves, the ones that have survived those conditions, and we must educate our young people.

When I speak of these deplorable conditions, please do not mistake what I am saying and assume that I mean it to apply only to the black race. I have spent the majority of my adult life in a cosmopolitan society. Since 1970, I have lived in Hawaii with the exception of five years between 1973 and 1978. I am interracially married with children and grandchildren that are interracial. I see people as individual human beings. Many are displaying good conduct, and many are displaying not-so-good conduct or behavior across all races and ethnic groups. Regrettably, I have seen far too many various ethnic groups experiencing the identical issues spoken about. These issues are not exclusive to black Americans. They exist among every race.

Please allow me to speak of the people of my state. Through my involvement with my fraternity and other social organizations, I became actively involved with multiracial groups within Hawaii. I gained what I feel to be useful knowledge that I would like to share. The people of Hawaii have learned a deep respect and appreciation for all cultures equally. They recognize and applaud the good qualities of the individual. They express feelings openly and easily with each other. They are warm and approachable. This includes the vast majority of our politicians. The dress for our business population is a neat, clean, and comfortable shirt and dress slacks. We are considered laid-back compared to many of the mainland business population.

The people of Hawaii say, "Aloha," which has many meanings, but each of them communicates "welcome as a friend, and peace be with you." This message is communicated in a friendly manner. As the leader of several of my social organizations, I met with the heads of other social organizations. We worked together to eliminate many of the adverse social conditions within our communities. This association presented an opportunity for me to contribute to others in a manner that was fulfilling. It was while doing much of this volunteer work that I became aware of many disturbing things. I began to really notice the different behavior patterns of people living in different neighborhoods.

Although I was born poor to sharecropper parents and have lived and worked in economically depressed neighborhoods, I had not gained an appreciation for the differences of behavior of people living in different communities. I have often asked myself why I had not noticed the differences before. As I attempted to find the answers to this question, several things began to become clear within my mind. First and foremost is that one's awareness of conditions depends on one's exposure to different environments.

Children who have grown up in poverty and who have never sat at a dinner table with fine china and linen will feel ill at ease the first time they are exposed to the environment. Those same children, when exposed to children who are dressed in the latest fashion, will feel uneasy. Those same children build a self-consciousness of their scarcity compared to other children. Those same children left unexposed to other environments have no self-awareness of their condition until exposed to other environments.

Of course we have televisions, computers, and every electronic game imaginable. For many children living in impoverished conditions, these things are only a fantasy—dreams that seem unobtainable. Once they are exposed to a different environment and allowed to adjust to it, the vast majority develops well.

Many of these children need nothing more than a mentor—someone who understands their conditions—to go into those economically depressed neighborhoods and show them the way out. There are several social organizations dedicated to the betterment of these children. The members of these organizations are not wealthy people. The majority are considered middle class, making just enough to support their families and educate their children.

Throughout I have asked fathers and young men to become actively involved in helping to change deviant behavior amongst the youth of our communities. It's essential that it be younger fathers, because teenagers cannot relate to men who have adult children comfortably. There is a language barrier between age groups, and young fathers relate much better than grandpa's does. I will share an example of what I mean a young man in his late twenties, who was a member of one of my fraternities, called my house one evening and ask to speak with me. When I told him he was speaking to me, he said, "What's-up dog?" My first thought was you don't know me, why call me a dog. I knew he was attempting to make a friendly connection and for his generation he was asking how you are friend.

There is a more compelling reason that it be young fathers, not only do you communicate easier, teenagers are easily impressed by middle age men much more than by grandfathers. They respect grandfathers and love talking to us but its young fathers that coaches various sports teams. It's the younger fathers' that play various sports with them, and you are the only ones who has the knowledge and energy enough to make the changes need in our economic depressed communities.

Effects of Poverty

For years I have known that poverty is not the affliction of blacks only—that it applies to every race within the United States. I have been to several countries and have seen poverty in some of them, but I never realized the awful impact poverty has on children until I became involved within those communities.

Growing up on those sharecropper farms in Georgia was one type of poverty. However, the poverty I grew up under was nothing compared to the poverty many of our young people are living under. To this date, I cannot ever remember being hungry. I can remember many unpleasant things, including the "less than" feeling. I can empathize with the feeling of "Why me?" I cannot, however, relate to the emotions that many of our depressed neighborhood children feel.

Many of these children are growing up in one-parent homes; others are in dysfunctional homes where family members are addicted to drugs. Many of these children are exposed to environments that are unimaginable to a large segment of our society. In my early twenties, I was involved with children. Many of them came from one-parent homes in depressed neighborhoods. However, they were clean, their clothes were clean, and their hair was neatly cared for. Their clothes were not fashionable, but as I recall, those kids appeared to be cared for.

It appears to me that over the past couple of decades, the effects of poverty have magnified themselves on a much greater scale within our society. Poverty conditions are found within every region of our nation. This brings me to my motivator for writing this book—New Orleans and Hurricane Katrina. It took this disaster to really open my eyes as well as my mind. As I watched television and saw the masses of people huddled around the convention center and the superdome, the one commonality they appeared to share was that they were people of very limited resources.

Many of those people had no means of evacuating themselves and had to rely on government officials. This reliance proved to be devastating for some. This reliance proved to be even deadly for others who could not get to the Superdome or any other safe place. The city of New Orleans is one that advertises its charm, entertainment, and fun, and it is a city my wife and I found to be friendly, entertaining, and beautiful. A city of enchantment was placed on display by this terrible disaster for the world to see.

Hurricane Katrina displayed to the world the inequities of societies that place greater emphasis on wealth, entertainment, and pleasure than on the welfare of their citizens. Many reading this statement will come to the conclusion that I am delirious and that this statement is completely false. Perhaps this is a false assumption on my behalf, but I ask that we consider my next comments.

Immediately following Hurricane Katrina, one of the first places to be restored was the New Orleans Superdome. This facility was seen as a necessity for the recovery of the city. What happened to the philosophy that *people* determine the direction of a city or state? The vast majority of those displaced and who had their homes destroyed by this disaster could not afford the price of a ticket to see the football team play in person. The only way many of those who lost their homes could afford to see their city's proud football team was by working the concessions stands carrying beer and snacks throughout the stadium.

From my perspective, the first objective should have been to use every available asset to rebuild those residential areas destroyed by the hurricane. People need employment, and cities need revenue. In my opinion, more employment and revenue would have been generated from the reconstruction of the destroyed areas than could be generated from revenue gained through sports that are played for six months a year. More important than the revenue generated from a sport team or reconstruction is the impact on the human being.

Are not people the greatest asset to any city or nation? My realities of life may be somewhat skewed by the environments I have been associated with. If so, then I make no apology, for within those environments, there was a belief that with hard work and obedience to the laws of society, one could reach his or her full potential as an individual. In reality, this premise has proven to be false for some. It is a great premise to believe in, but for many, the reality has been devastating.

Millions of Americans are questioning the above premise of working hard, obeying our laws, and relying on our economic system and our government to adequately provide for our needs. Many question a system that requests that everyone contribute as much as individually possible, yet rewards less than 5 percent of the nation's population with such a great proportion of the nation's wealth.

How does one justify any individual making in excess of fifty million dollars per year when others of the same organization are making less than fifty thousand? Does not this individual making fifty million per year share the responsibility to ensure that those with fewer abilities are adequately provided for? How does a nation, the wealthiest in the world, have millions without adequate health insurance? How does a nation, the wealthiest in the world, have millions living in poverty? How does this same nation have more of its citizens incarcerated than other industrialized, civilized nations? This same nation is said to have the second-largest number of billionaires in the world.

Did these billionaires create those billions themselves? Did not millions of Americans assist them in their accumulation? Of course these billionaires had the creative ideas and deserve tremendous reward for their creativity. In my opinion, the greatest creators of the world needed others to realize the potential for their creativity. Should they not reward those involved fairly?

As I associated with different organizations and cultures, intermingling with the various nationalities, I became more acutely aware that every culture and nationality I

intermingled with shared the same aspirations—to house, feed, clothe, and educate their younger generations, to purchase houses and make homes, and to earn decent livings, all while hoping for healthy lives with fairly comfortable retirements in the twilight years of their lives. I discovered that, regardless of the color of their skin, majority want to live in peaceful, law-abiding neighborhoods, see their children and grandchildren receive a good education, and enjoy the benefits of a good, healthy life.

During this period, I began to focus on the mass complexity of societies and governments that are established to control the masses. The intricacy of societies living together in peace and harmony requires intense cooperation, combined with extensive training with the execution of good judgment. We the citizens of the United States of America have a system of government established to operate in such a manner.

We elect those we believe will work most effectively at complying with the wishes of our communities. We place many of these people into office to discover to our dismay that they were lacking in ability, yet we continue to reelect them. Does this practice seem logical to many of you? We elect these inept officials at every level of government and continue to return them to office. Why?

Many will argue that they are good politicians. What is a good politician? Is not a good politician one who places the majority interest of constituents above all else at the local level and the majority of national interest at the federal level? Do you and I not have a stake in the governance of our society at all levels of government?

Do we not have an obligation to contribute positively in whatever way possible? Our communities need and require more men like those of us who have found a way to break the cycle of poverty to be educators within our communities. Not only must we be educators within our communities, but we must be active participants within our political system.

As stated, we elect many inept officials and continue to reelect them. We have another phenomenal trend—we keep reelecting individuals into political office that have lived well into the twilight years of their lives. These individuals are tremendous citizens of our nation; they are loyal and dedicated. Many of this group earned our gratitude, and several have my gratitude and respect.

There is great wisdom among our nation's political citizens in their twilight years. When reflecting upon their political careers, one cannot help but feel a sense of pride about their contributions to our nation. Yet, I question the rationale of people electing political leaders who are into their eighties.

My questioning is not of their mental ability, but of their stamina. In many professions, age limits are imposed because of the limitation age places on one's stamina. Managing public affairs requires much stamina and a tremendous intellectual mind with a burning desire to serve people. Many of these elected officials in their twilight years would better serve their nation by retiring, allowing younger, more energetic people to serve.

We live in a complicated world. There is much poverty, many wars, and people destroying each other for no reason other than greed and twisted ideology. Peoples of all nations are coming to this country. Others are depending on America for leadership. One of this nation's most treasured monuments has the following sonnet written by Emma Lazarus engraved on a tablet inside its pedestal:

> Not like the brazen giant of Greek fame, With conquering limbs astride from land to land; Here at our sea-washed, sunset gates shall stand A mighty woman with a torch, whose flame Is the imprisoned lightning, and her name Mother of Exiles. From her beacon-hand Glows world-wide welcome; her mild eyes command The air-bridged harbor that twin cities frame. "Keep, ancient lands, your storied pomp!" cries she With silent lips. "Give me your tired, your poor,
> Your huddled masses yearning to breathe free,
> The wretched refused of your teeming shore.
> Send these, the homeless, tempest-toss to me,
> I lift my lamp besides the golden door!"

This sonnet is supposed to be representative of our nation and our beliefs, as we are a country of immigrants of all nationalities that have come together. We believe in "The American's Creed" as written by William Tyler Page in 1917 and acknowledged and accepted by the United States House of Representatives on April 3, 1918, which reads:

> I believe in the United States of America as a government of the people, by the people, for the people; whose just powers are derived from the consent of the governed; a democracy in a republic; a sovereign Nation of many sovereign

> States; a perfect union, one and inseparable; established upon those principles of freedom, equality, justice, and humanity for which American patriots sacrificed their lives and fortunes. I therefore believe it is my duty to my country to love it, to support its Constitution, to obey its laws, to respect its flag, and to defend it against all enemies.

Millions of Americans—including myself—literally believe in the message of the above document. There are times when I feel that many of our political leaders have forgotten this message. I think they believe in the message but have become overwhelmed by power and the association of wealth to the point that they have forgotten the common and less influential citizens of our states and nation. Americans, we need to raise our voices; it's the only way we are going to be heard.

Tremendously Dedicated Americans Assisting Their Communities

Fathers, I have appealed to you throughout this book. I have asked that many of us reexamine our roles within our family structure and within our communities. Now I wish to share my experiences with a group of men that are super fathers. Many of these men are members of several different social organizations. These men belong to every profession within our society. They believe in their deity, their country, their families, their neighbors, and themselves.

These men make numerous contributions to the citizens of our nation. Several of these men have come out of many of these economically depressed, segregated communities. They are our seniors, men with a great understanding of the characteristics and needs of these communities. These men were and are the backbones of black economically depressed communities. They are advocates of good education and government. Much of the progress made in these communities can be directly attributed to members of this organization.

There are other organizations making tremendous contributions to our economically depressed communities. I will not mention any specific organization by name. I have been a member of this one particular organization for almost forty plus years. I am personally familiar with and knowledgeable of this outstanding organization's contributions to these economically depressed communities and our nation.

Members of this organization will recognize themselves as I speak of their contributions within our communities. To you, the members of this organization, I am convinced that we must revisit our purpose as an organization. We must also redefine the definition of one of our obligations. The obligation that says we are to protect our widows and orphans. Today, our widows are no longer the wives of the deceased. They are our single mothers, birthing babies and remaining single, often caring for that baby or babies alone. Many of today's widows have not become adults, yet others have become grandmother widows before the age of thirty. It is not these widows who concern me. It is the orphans of these widows.

These orphans are being neglected, mistreated, and abused, many by their mothers and others by their mothers' sleepover sex partners. To the members of this organization, your forefathers came together and worked in unity with leaders of communities to eliminate many of the adverse conditions of their time. I realize that our membership is not as great as it once was, but I sincerely believe that we must continue to show a physical connection within our depressed communities. We must open our churches and meeting halls to these at-risk children. We must establish tutoring classes and solicit for volunteer instructors. We give away thousands of dollars annually in scholarships to worthy children. I suggest that we publicize the offering of scholarships to high school students who will come forward and tutor needy youths.

You should be commended for your contributions to educating our young people, and I sincerely commend each of you. Times require that we be much more creative in the expenditure of our funds. My comments and suggestions are offered for debate and are not intended as a solution. If I had the solutions, I would be wealthy, and many of our communities would be in better condition.

This new category of widows and orphans has created a paradigm shift to which we have not yet adjusted. It is important that we analyze our effectiveness within these communities. We must mentor these young male orphans to becoming respectful, contributing citizens on reaching adulthood. We must teach them to break the cycle of being sperm donors for this category of widows.

We must teach our sons that if it is a necessity to become sperm donors for these women, they must have an understanding with the women. They must make it known that they expect to be equally and actively involved in the child's life in a positive way. If necessary, we might need to inform these young women, if they have the need to be sexually active, that they must use birth control methods until they are able to care for and support a child.

To the members of this organization, again, thank you for your contributions. You have been beacons of light for our disadvantaged young people. Let us unite in constructive dialogue with leaders of other community organizations to assist us in eradicating much of the destructive behavior demonstrated by many of our young people. We have a membership reported to be in excess of three hundred thousand. If we unite, think of the additional contributions we can make.

For those educated with influential positions within our society, please gather men of similar abilities. Come together and formulate a plan—one that we as an organization can implement at the community level to aggressively engage community issues. Many of us have commented on the decline of membership over the years. I believe that if we solidify ourselves in creating positive changes within these communities, our membership will greatly increase.

Can you visualize the positive impact that we can have in these neighborhoods that are dominated primarily by single mothers? Children of every race are displaying deviant and destructive behavior. The consequences of this behavior have affected the black race disproportionately. To you, my friends, thank you for your contributions.

Lessons Learned As a City Bus Driver

Allow me to talk more about my occupation as a bus operator for the City and County of Honolulu and the valuable lessons I learned. Earlier I stated that, had someone suggested that I pursue a career as a bus driver, I would have said, "No, thank you." However, after having failed to successfully grow my business, I had to seek employment.

One of my friends was employed at the bus company as a dispatch supervisor. I mentioned to him that I would be closing my company within three months, as that would be the end of my obligation on my last contract. He informed me that the bus company was hiring and asked me if I had ever considered driving a bus. Of course, my answer was no. But I knew that I had to find employment to assist my wife in maintaining the standard of living we had become accustomed to living.

This friend explained the salary and benefits offered by the company that managed the system. After hearing the information, I decided to apply. As I said earlier, I was confident that, with my experiences, I would be hired. What was surprising for me was the starting salary. It was as good as my top salary while in the military.

Not only was the salary as good, the fringe benefit package was as good as the military's benefits. We had one month of paid vacation per year, fifteen days of paid sick leave, and full medical coverage. The medical coverage covered employee and family members without employee financial contribution. In addition, this company provided a good retirement plan through the Teamsters Union. The lesson I learned here was that one should investigate various opportunities before forming an opinion. Many times, things are not as we perceive them to be.

My perception of city bus operators was different from my perception of truck drivers and interstate bus operators. To me, the latter ones traveled to different states, enhancing their appeal. I enjoy traveling and meeting different cultures. My father was an interstate truck driver and often carried me on trips with him during summer months.

My only exposure to city buses was of those I had ridden as a teenager in Savannah, Georgia. Those bus rides had not left a favorable impression upon me. Remember, I grew up in a segregated period—a period where, if you were black, it was "Move to the back." On many of those bus rides, there would be plenty of seats, but the bus would be separated by race. Many whites would go three-quarters of the way to the rear of the bus and sit intentionally to force blacks to stand because blacks could not sit in front of whites. My environment!

In today's world and in the world in which I became a bus operator, no one cares where anyone sits. I had ridden on other forms of public transportation without forming any opinions of those systems. Why had I formed an opinion about city buses? I did not know, and I had not thought on the subject until after I became a bus operator.

After driving the bus for a short period of time, I began to notice symptoms of behavior displayed by certain segments of the population of Hawaii—behavior that I had observed in those segregated neighborhoods I grew up in. These symptoms were and are being displayed by every race and culture. Not only were these symptoms displayed by the adults, they were also displayed by the young people and adolescents, and often to an even greater degree. My observations of what I perceived to be destructive behavior began to tug at my conscience.

For most of my adult life, I had been involved in some small way of helping the youth. I had removed myself from those economically depressed communities. I would go back in for a few hours, but I had not really seen this population. This bothered me, as I had no additional time to volunteer, and I was already expending as much time as possible. The voluntary work I was doing would benefit only a few children. As I'd had good relations with this population and had worked well with the youth over the years, I wondered how I could better contribute.

My wife must have noticed my frustration. She came to me and said, "You have always said you were going back to college!" I had started college immediately after retiring from the army but dropped out because of the time required in establishing my business. While establishing the business, I was also the president of the local chapter of my fraternal organization. Her reminder came at the appropriate time. I had been at the bus company long enough; I was familiar with all the routes and had a good knowledge of a bus operator's duties.

The day after our conversation, I went to one of our junior colleges and enrolled as a beginning student. I could have had credits granted me for military training and life experiences, but I chose to start as our children had—as a freshman without any credits. As you have already read, I took a full load, which led to my bachelor's degree in social sciences.

What were the symptoms of behavior that I had observed that bothered me? Many of the young men were boisterous, ill mannered, impolite, and traveled in packs displaying identical conduct. These packs would often ride the bus during school hours. When questioned as to why they were not in school, there was no limit to their excuses. None of the excuses were authorized by a parent or school official.

The use of profanity among this group is appalling. They use it in front of small children, male or female. These young men use profanity around women old enough to be their grandmothers without any appearance of respect. I grew up seeing behavior of this type. I worked in communities where youngsters displayed this type of behavior. My observation of the major differences between these groups and groups I grew up and worked among was their disrespectful, vulgar use of language around seniors and women.

Fathers, many of these young men are asking for attention. They don't have male role models in their lives to demonstrate the manner in which they should try to live. These young men need guidance. Let me share things and techniques I employed when dealing with this group. If they were just rowdy, I would stop the bus in a secure bus stop, dismount my seat, walk to where they were sitting, and say in a polite manner, "Excuse me. I want to ask you guys to do me a favor. Please hold down on the volume and the use of profanity. We have elder women and young children aboard for whom your language is inappropriate." They would respond with, "Yeah, sure, man," 80 percent of the time, and sometimes the volume would go back up. I would look in the rearview mirror and raise my index finger in the air, shaking it. Many times, it would be all that was required.

About 10 percent of the time, these groups would—in unintelligent language—inform me of what I could do with my request. On those occasions, I would return to my seat and commence driving. At the same time, I called for police assistance to meet me and remove them from the bus. The other 10 percent of the time, I would call the police without approaching them—period. Many of the latter group displayed violent behavior and mannerisms. Bus drivers who avoided getting assaulted have the ability to recognize this behavior and the intelligence enough to call for assistance when needed.

An incident happened one night at about eleven o'clock. I was driving a route that services an area of our state that has the second-largest number of high school dropouts. This area also has more unemployed and homeless people than any other section of my state.

Anyway, on this night, a group of approximately eight teenage boys boarded my bus, paid their fare, and went to the rear of the bus. Once we reached the terminus and I had turned around, reversing my route, the young fellows were still on. I pulled up to the beach park, went to use the restroom, and returned to the bus. The young men were still aboard. I went to the rear and asked their destination. One of them said, "We are cruising." I informed them that it would require another fare, as we had reached the end of the line. This same young fellow said, "We are not paying, and we are going to ride back." I returned to the driver's compartment and retrieved my metal transfer punch to use as a weapon should the need occur. I then reached over and picked up my radio receiver, pressing the button for assistance while keeping my back to the driver's compartment with my body facing them.

They got up out of their seats and approached me. One of the fellows said, "You called the police on us, huh?" I informed him that I had. He said, "I should go up side your head." Without looking away or raising my voice, I said to them, "Someone's mother will visit a hospital tonight." They looked at each other and started walking off the bus. Once on the outside, they started mumbling and using profanity, but they walked off in the opposite direction.

There were a couple of young men sitting in a car parked nearby. They came over to the bus after the group started walking away and said, "We saw what was happening and would have come to your defense had they assaulted you." I thanked them for their concern.

The group continued walking away. I received a call from my central control office requesting the type of assistance I needed. I explained the incident and was questioned as to my safety. Central control informed me that this group had most of the drivers on that shift afraid of them. They had been intimidating drivers, riding free, and getting off the bus prior to the police intercepting the bus in route.

They inquired as to why I was not afraid. I informed them that I did feel uneasy. That is why I had gotten the metal transfer punch. I also knew I could not stop them from doing something they were intent on doing. The only thing I could do was ensure that they knew I understood, and that I was willing to make one or two of them pay a tremendous price, should they have assaulted me. Would I have done this had these fellows been older? Probably not. Was it an intelligent thing to do? Probably not. There are times when we must confront deviant behavior displayed by our young people. It is one of our responsibilities as adult men of our communities.

Over the years, I have often confronted deviant behavior that other adults have ignored. Several of my friends and acquaintances have suggested that the reason I have not had any adverse repercussions from confronting individuals exhibiting such behavior is because of my voice. I have a very deep voice. Many have said it sounds like James Earl Jones's voice. Others say I sound like Lou Rawls. I don't know what I sound like, only that if I speak in a crowd; my voice seems to attract attention.

Maybe there is something unique about my voice. My mother had Alzheimer's disease years before she died. She could not remember my name, but she could remember my voice. I would call her and ask if she knew me. Her answer would always be, "Who don't know that voice?" So maybe there is something with the voice.

Regrettably, I saw teenage girls and young women displaying similar behavior. Their numbers were small compared to the male population. However, allow me to share a few of my observations of a large number of our young females of these economically depressed neighborhoods. Before I share them, please note that I am not specifying any particular race. I live in Hawaii, and this state has a multitude of ethnic groups. These behaviors are exhibited daily and in increasing numbers among this group of young women.

These young women often skip school like their male counterparts. They give the appearance of enjoying overexposing the nudity of their bodies. Many are loud and have a mouthful of chewing gum, popping it in everyone's ears. Many of their young faces are painted to the point of absurdity in their attempts to beautify themselves. Many of these girls are beautiful and need no makeup. The vast majority of these youngsters are good girls searching for love and attention.

Another trend of these young girls, many as young as thirteen or fourteen years old, is that they display sexual behavior. Their clothes are scanty, and they are crawling all over some boy or young man, as if they are prepared to have sex in public. We know the results of behavior of this nature. Fathers and men, we can improve conduct of this type. We must give these girls the love of male attention that they are seeking. Many of these young women have never had a male relative tell them how pretty they are and how much they are loved. I know many of you fathers are asking, what does this have to do with me? The girl is not my daughter.

Fathers and men, many of the young men that these girls are becoming involved with are our sons. Do we not have an obligation to teach our sons and young men decent values? Should we not teach responsibility? When my sons were about ten and twelve, thinking that I was a modern-day parent, I decided it was time to talk with them about sex.

After everything I said, they would reply, "We know that already." I inquired as to where they were getting their information. They said that they were getting it in health class at school. I thought to myself, thanks for a good educational program at their school, apparently, I'm not as modern of a father as I think I am.

Therefore, I said to them, "I want to tell you something that the school has not taught you. When either of you start having sex with a young woman, be sure they are on birth control, and you are using condoms. If the young woman becomes pregnant, you have a child. I don't want to hear that I have a grandchild or that the child is not yours. If you think enough of the person to have sex without protecting yourself, to me you trust and respect the person."

"Please understand me; I am not saying you and the woman have an obligation to marry each other. However, both of you share the obligation of raising your child. The child is the innocent one. You and the young woman have committed no crime. You have, however, bonded yourself together to a precious gift for life. These are my feelings. It's your life. Having children is a tremendous responsibility, but also a tremendous joy."

"If the young woman has a reputation that would make you ashamed to bring her to family dinners or special occasions with your family, then I strongly suggest that you not have unprotected sex with her. You should never have unprotected sex, period, unless you are prepared to commit to each other."

On many of those bus routes, we were required to transport school-aged youths to their schools. Several bus operators would complain about the rowdiness of the youths who were catching their buses. On my off days, when other operators would drive my route, they would compliment the conduct of the passengers.

Many would ask me what my technique was for keeping them under control. I explained that I did not try to control them. Upon my first interaction with the students, I would explain what I considered to be appropriate conduct aboard my bus. I explained to the kids that they had options—they could obey the rules as I had stated them or catch the following bus. Often, the first time I would pull up to a bus stop after school, a crowd of children would be waiting and shoveling each other to board the bus first. After stopping, I would sit with the door closed until they settled down.

What I discovered was that, by sitting there with the door closed, many would yell, and some would even use profanity, yet they would soon line up behind each other without me saying anything. Once their behavior had calmed down, I would get up from my seat, open the door, and address the students as to what I expected their behavior to be.

Without an exception, these children would follow the rules. For those that had used profanity, I addressed their behavior by informing them that, on my bus, profanity was not used, and should I identify someone using profanity, they would be asked to remove themselves from the bus. These children were noisy and playful. To me, there is nothing wrong with being noisy and playful; they are children. I want children to be cheerful and enjoy one another. I also want them to be respectful of themselves and of others. We the adults must teach this, especially fathers; we are the authoritarian figures in these young lives.

Fathers, we have much to do to assist our children, especially those in our economically depressed communities. Grandpas, we need to raise our voices with regard to these conditions. Many of our younger generations have not experienced our conditions. Thanks to the efforts of millions of us, our children and grandchildren did not have to confront conditions many of us lived under. I swell with pride when I see many of my ethnic group's positive contributions to every institution within our nation.

Is that not what Dr. Martin Luther King Jr. died for? Not only did Dr. King die, but many others did, too. Dr. King asked for us to bury this race issue and see ourselves as humans of equals. The progress made in seeing ourselves as equals over the last forty years has improved greatly, but we have much further to go.

As I drove those city buses, I observed other trends of behavior I had seen previously. One of those trends was class, or what one perceives as his or her class. What drew my attention to this behavior were the mannerisms of a specific group of passengers. All of these passengers were employed and lived within the same community.

Observing their behavior was curiously interesting to me. These passengers would automatically intermingle into small groups. Their intermingling into small groups reflected their occupations. It was very obvious which among the groups were those employed within white-collar occupations, such as professional, governmental agencies, and administrative fields. These people would often not speak to me or to those employed within the blue-collar occupations, such as hotel and service industry employees, construction workers, carpenters, and trade union employees. This behavior was more noticeable on the "express buses." Express buses are buses that service a particular community and then proceed by the most direct route to a central employment district. Once someone of either group started a dialogue with someone in the other group, I would see friendships develop.

This behavior caused me to reflect back on my experiences of intermingling with people. As I reflected back on my life, I realized that I had exhibited those signs. In my case, those white-collar and professional employees intimidated me. What did they do to intimidate me? Nothing—they reminded me of who I thought I wanted to become. To me, they represented intelligence and success. The neatness of their dress impressed me. They represented a good house and a better salary than I had.

My clothes were always clean and pressed but not necessarily of the latest fashion. My life, having begun under impoverished conditions, had caused me to feel inferior to certain people. I was uneasy when talking to professional people. I felt that I could not carry on an intelligible conversation. I did not feel that I had the educational training to communicate well; these were my feelings for years. Around blue-collar workers, I felt comfortable. I grew up around farmers, plumbers, and truck drivers. I talked with them every day. If my language was bad, so what? We spoke the same language. Again, it is about one's *environment!*

Once someone in a white-collar profession opened a conversation with me, I was forced to respond. Over a period of time, I became more at ease communicating with professional people. If "normal" adults are exhibiting this sort of behavior, what can we expect from our homeless, malnourished, and economically depressed children?

The behavior of many of those passengers aboard the express buses was a direct reflection of my past behavior. The knowledge gained from this observation was interesting to me. Many of those blue-collar workers lived in larger homes than many of the white-collar workers. Many had luxury automobiles parked in their yards, and several had college degrees. Yet it appeared that many held the same perception I held—that a neatly dressed and manicured person was somehow different.

One of my opinions of this group of people representing professional occupations was that they thought that they were superior to me. Was this true? Of course some of them did, but the vast majority of them did not. I also observed that once the connection was made between the two groups, there would be smiles on their faces and pleasant conversations among them.

How had I come to the above conclusion? When spoken to first, many in the above category would mumble, look away or down, and very seldom would they look me in the eye. This behavior was confusing. To me, it said, "I don't have time to look in your direction," or "How dare you interrupt my thoughts by speaking to me?" I had not consciously recalled the above feeling for several years, factually speaking—not since the late 1970s or early 1980s. This observation on the buses was in the late 1990s and 2000s. In my earlier years, I was conditioned by my environment to expect and accept those feelings as being a part of my life.

This observation and my interpretation of it could be wrong. My objective of bringing it up is to get you, the reader, to think about little signals displayed among us daily by our young people. Many of our children feel uncomfortable going to our public schools. Why? Because their parents cannot afford to buy the latest fashions in clothes for them to wear. Many feel embarrassed and find difficulty in socializing with other children.

Within this child's mind, he or she doesn't feel equal to the well-dressed child. If you question this, I suggest that you spend a little voluntary time at your local school and observe the children's behavior. I think you will find that those dressed in the latest fashions will congregate together, and those who are not will congregate together. Most parents recognize this. Many will burden themselves attempting to purchase the latest fashion in clothes for their kids because they want them to be accepted as equals.

Over the years, I have spent a considerable amount of time in other countries. In several of these countries, I observed that the younger children going to school were dressed in uniform. I didn't give much thought to this subject until I began volunteer teaching at a school for youth at risk. After thinking over the subject, it drew my focus on parochial schools within the United States. From my observation, the vast majority of parochial schools require that the students wear uniforms.

The more I thought on the subject, the more I became fond of the idea of elementary and secondary grade students being required to wear uniforms. To me, this places the children on an equal footing—all are there to get an education. Will this stop kids from forming their own little cliques because of superficial things like dress? No, this will not stop cliques from being formed. However, they will be formed based on shared personalities or interests.

Fathers, those of us who have improved our life conditions, regardless of our status or class, had someone's help and encouragement. Many of the children in our economically depressed neighborhoods need a hand to reach out and touch them. Many of these children require much more, and many of their parents need our help. In many cases, we expend millions of dollars on programs to change these children's behavior, yet expend nothing, not even effort, to change the casual factors of their behavior—their parents and their environment.

During this period of employment as a bus operator, I had succeeded in removing myself from living among our economically depressed neighborhoods. I had made a successful military career and had learned to feel comfortable communicating with field grade officers from the rank of major through general. I had operated my own business for a period, communicating with executives of various levels, and had acquired a college degree. I had associated with professionals of various fields—medical, judicial, political, and business.

Over the years, I had become immune to the effects that our behavior has on certain members of society. Seeing this behavior recalled memories that were unpleasant for me in my younger years. I pondered my feelings and recognized that, even after many years, aspects of the environment to which I was exposed as a very young child were still embedded within my subconscious mind. I have worked hard to erase those feelings and know that they are unhealthy for me, but there are occasions when others' actions bring back bad memories.

Working as a bus operator provided me the unique opportunity to analyze the behavior of different cultures, genders, and age groups. In addition to providing the opportunity for analyzing different cultures and groups, this employment provided me with an opportunity to analyze a large nonprofit management firm.

The study of this firm and my elected position as state president of my fraternal organization eventually led me to the field in which I pursued my graduate studies degree—more about this later. I applied for and received an appointment to the position of temporary dispatcher with the bus company. In that position, I discovered what I considered to be the negative ramifications of employees being assigned to duties for which they are unqualified.

It was a tremendous opportunity for gaining insight into the various ethnic traditions among the people of the islands. This employment and my leadership positions within my fraternal organizations also provided me with insight about myself. After retiring from this employment, I decided to return to college again, this time to earn my master's degree. I earned my Master of Science in administration, with a concentration in public administration, a month before my sixty-seventh birthday.

This book began because of the hurt and sadness I felt after seeing the devastating effects Hurricane Katrina had on the people of New Orleans and the Mississippi Gulf Coast. After beginning this book, several of our nation's economic problems have been exposed, and they require attention and assiduous efforts on the part of many. In my opinion, these economic problems will adversely affect many Americans-black American to a greater extent than most. Our history tells us that if you are of the black race, unemployment in prosperous times is greatest among this race than any other. Our history also tells us that there are large discrepancies in salaries earned for doing comparable jobs.

Many are aware that the black unemployment rate in late 2005 and early 2006 was more than double that of the white race (10.6 compared to 4.3 percent). This was before the revelation of the unpleasant condition our nation's economy is presently in. I'm afraid that the coming years are going to place much of our nation's population, especially those at the lower economic level, under tremendous stress.

Our young people are the first to feel the greatest impact of adverse conditions. The impact of our current economic conditions will affect some aspect of every Americans life. My concern is not for black Americans, but all Americans, and my heart aches when I think of the affect on many of our children.

Racism and Its Repulsive Connotations

At the beginning, I stated it is my belief Race and Class, played a significant role in the lack of immediate response of emergency measures to aid many victims of Hurricane Katrina. Please allow me to express my feelings about Race. Something happened after I began writing this book. From my perspective, this event has been one of the most important events of my lifetime. Never have I been more proud of our Nation. Many of our citizens came together and selected an outstanding young man to head the National Democratic Party as its Presidential Candidate his name is Barack Obama.

Please note that I did not specify a race. Why? Because to me, this young man is not of a black or white race; he is multiracial. When he first began to run for the presidency of the United States, one of the first questions that was raised and aired over the news media was, is he black enough? This was later followed by the statement that he is the first African American to be elected to head the Democratic Party as its presidential candidate.

These statements began to represent to me many disturbing images of past experiences—images of experiences I'd hoped had long been buried. Who cares whether Senator Obama is of a particular race? Black Americans, we have a right to feel proud of Senator Obama's achievements. Are not his achievements what previous generations of our ethnic group fought and many died for? If we work for the dream, apply ourselves, get a good education, and do good to all mankind, the dream is achievable. Are not these the dreams of all Americans? Many people have lost their lives trying to reach our shores to accomplish their dreams.

What disturbed me is that race was immediately a topic of this election process by both blacks and whites. What does one mean when he or she asks, "Is he black enough?" Are there any specific characteristics about one being black? Are we implying that he has not prostituted our women or that he is not one of the criminal justice system's statistics? Does one need characteristics like those mentioned above? It seems to me that those are characteristics of blacks displayed predominantly over the news media. Because he does not share these characteristics, does it eliminate him from being black enough? It appears to me that we should be proudest of the fact that he does not share those characteristics.

Others were asking: Is he too black? Is he religious enough? Is he Muslim? Is he patriotic enough? Again, why should we care? Is not the intelligence of the individual more important? Is not the fact that he is inspirational and encouraging more important? Is not the fact that he is one of a selected few to have been elected as president of the Harvard Law Review a testimonial to his intelligence? Is not the fact he is a loyal United States citizen most important? To me, this young man brings a uniqueness of approach to solving problems.

President Obama began life under conditions he had no control over, the same as you and I. However, he had an additional predicament to overcome, one which deals with America's darkest history—one of the slave and that of the enslaver (black and white). His parents had committed an unforgivable act for many—a black man and white woman marrying each other. Many of you are probably beginning to think, *this guy is nuts.* Please bear with me and read my opinions. Many will disagree with me. I respect this, but I'm writing about my experiences.

America's history is blotted with the blood of black men who were killed because they were perceived to have spoken to or looked at a white woman in a manner not approved of by white men. To speak to a white woman in a friendly manner was once considered to be a death sentence for black men.

Not only was it a death sentence for black men, but also for black male youths as exemplified by the death of fourteen-year-old Emmett Till. President Obama grew up hearing both blacks and whites making derogatory remarks about one another. One would think that those comments had to be hurtful to him. He had a natural love for both his parents; they were not black or white to him. They were "Mom" and "Dad."

This interracial childhood and growing up in a cosmopolitan society afforded this man an insight into ethnic backgrounds that is not shared by a majority of our nation. To me, this is to his advantage. He grew up in a society in which blacks and whites were minorities. He learned at a very young age that all races are important. One must be able to communicate with multiple races and nationalities.

He attended one of Hawaii's most prestigious schools, which was and is integrated with every ethnic group imaginable. Hawaii is a state made up of every culture within the world. Those cultures that do not reside within the state are here daily throughout the year on vacation. One becomes accustomed to listening closely to others and building coalitions with various groups. This value was instilled within President Obama growing up in Hawaii while he was playing basketball and other sports. There were no black or white basketball teams. They were basketball teams consisting of a majority of Polynesians, Asians, and Indonesians.

My point is that President Obama learned these things as a child. It comes naturally for him to build coalitions with various ethnic groups to accomplish things. Remember, I stated earlier that Hawaii is better than any state I have lived in or visited for cultures living, intermingling, and cooperating together while maintaining culture traditions. He has been accused of displaying an elitist attitude. How can one look at someone of a broken interracial home, whose mother had to rely on welfare for a period, and accuse that person of being an elitist?

Many have referred to this gentleman as being young and inexperienced. I ask: Is forty-seven years old considered young? Experienced? Experienced at what? Many of our politicians' have much more political experience than President Obama, yet they have failed to accomplish any great deeds for our nation. When I hear a political person referencing age or one's youth and experience, I often think of a man who was assassinated before he was forty years old. This man had won the Noble Peace Prize, and his contributions forced a nation to closely examine itself and change some of the most racist and suppressive laws of any nation.

This same man was beaten, jailed, spied on, and his character was defamed by our governmental law enforcement officials and many politicians. This man, a man who has a national holiday in honor of him and of his worthy contributions to the United States and humanity, was Dr. Martin Luther King Jr.

President Obama, frequently cited for having written an inspiring book, delivers motivating and exciting speeches. Ask yourself what it was that Dr. King did. He gave motivational and inspiring speeches. He was able to articulate the message of the average person in a manner that everyone could understand. He had the ability to communicate and feel with the people. This motivated the people to rise up against the unjust and the inhuman treatment afflicted against certain citizens of our nation.

President Obama has the ability to give motivational speeches. He is asking us as a nation to change our old ways and old habits and to look at things from a new and different perspective. We have lots of problems, America—a lot of problems—and he can articulate them. He has become what some—particularly his political opponents—call a celebrity. To me, that statement suggests that they are trying to say that he is a man who is famous without any substance. I don't see President Obama as being without substance. I see an intelligent, articulate, bright young man—a man who has no chip on his shoulder about his race or who he is. Not only does President Obama share the above attributes, he has a vision. Are not these attributes shared by individuals who have demonstrated outstanding leadership?

He commenced his journey under circumstances that are difficult for many of us to understand. His parents had committed a taboo for many Americans; a white woman had married a black man. Worst yet, this man—his father—abandoned both mom and child. President Obama went through school and graduated from one of our nation's most prestigious law schools. He was elected to head the Harvard Law Review.

Not only was he elected as one of the presidents of the school's law review, when he departed law school, he went back into a community completely different from Hawaii—a community where he had worked as an organizer, working to improve the conditions of the those who lived there. This community apparently knew him and was satisfied with his accomplishments; they elected him to serve as their state representative.

This was an accomplishment. It represents success, and it represents foresight coupled with intelligence. The people of his community saw and recognized his abilities. They sent him to their state senate. While serving in their state senate, the entire state observed him and saw his abilities. Apparently they thought, hey, here is a young man who is about something. He has the ability to think and the ability to reach out and touch others. He also encourages others to participate; he is inclusive. President Obama is not saying he has all the answers. He is saying, 'These are the problems, and we can overcome these problems if we tackle them together.

What is frustrating and bothersome for me about this issue is that, from my experiences, here is a young man who is saying, "These are the things I believe to be wrong, and these are my recommendations for fixing them. I don't have all the answers, but I am willing to sit across the table and talk with different people, different institutions, and different nations in search of correct answers." This young man said, "I am willing to talk; I am willing to listen." Isn't this what we ask of our leaders? Is this not what we asked our other elective representatives of Congress to do? Have we not asked them to listen, to work together, and, when necessary, to move across party lines for the good of our nation? I am mystified as to why more elective representatives do not do this. I am not the only one who feels this way; several of my friends and acquaintances tell me that they do also. Mine is only one voice. Speak out, America. Raise your voice—it matters!

Of course, by now it should have become obvious to you that I am a supporter of President Obama. I support him wholeheartedly as our president of the United States of America. Initially I supported Senator Hillary Clinton, whom our President exhibited his intelligence, leadership and courage in selecting Secretary of State. Initially I supported Secretary Clinton because she is a lady who I think have been tremendous for America and for all races. She has championed women issues, children's issues, health issues, education issues, and racial and economic issues.

She is an intelligent woman that has fought for many of the things I sincerely believe in. She has a record of fighting for the issues of people. As a result, she became the person I initially supported. I voted for her in my state's caucus. I sincerely believe with all my heart that she would have been an outstanding president for the country on the whole. There would have been some that she would not have pleased—nobody can.

Whether it be President Obama or anyone else, no one—man or woman—can please everybody. I don't think we want him to. However, *we want him to form a majority and work with that majority to solve our national problems.* I genuinely felt that Secretary Clinton would have done this. After the people spoke, I really started looking into then Senator Obama and listening to him talk. I began to realize that for the first time in many years, I could really say that we had very capable people running for the presidency of the United States who truly had a feel for the people.

What do I consider to be a feel for the people? It is having a comprehensive knowledge that *all* people are important. Not just selected groups, the entire mixture of people are what make the United States. It is what makes this country what it is, and unless we look out for all the people, we will have major problems. Our government must look out for all the people, but we—we the people—must speak out. We must become more involved in our community and government.

Please don't misread or misinterpret my message to imply that the other presidential candidate, Senator John McCain, is not an outstanding and tremendously dedicated American citizen. A man who every American should feel extremely proud of, this man has given a large portion of his life for this country, not only as a war veteran and hero, but as a senator, and these contributions should be commended, respected, and treasured by all Americans.

Senator McCain is one man. We were looking for a leader who has the vision to pursue the courses of action that are best for the majority of Americans, and we were looking for one who can bring about ideas. We had been and still is stagnated and gridlocked by political parties. America, we have problems—major problems—within our society. We see them, yet little has been done about them over the past few years.

Who can do something about them? Senator McCain said he can, but I disagreed with him. If he could have, he would have done it already. He would have found a way to have become much more vocal about many of our pressing issues in those twenty-six years in the Senate.

President Obama went into his U.S. Senate and noticed within a couple of years that it had become almost impossible to accomplish the things he felt were of the greatest importance for the nation. He noted that instead of discussing and solving issues that affected the majority of Americans, many of our elected officials had become bogged down in philosophical issues along party lines. He appears to be insightful enough to recognize that the majority of Americans are not locked into any one ideology. It seems to me that many of our political leaders lack the ability to place things into proper perspective.

America, it seems to me that we have political leaders who appear to be more concerned about their religious beliefs and indoctrination than the welfare of our nation. One's religious belief or indoctrination has no place on the public agenda. I, too, believe in Jesus Christ and God. It's my personal faith; I use it to guide my private and public actions. My understanding of religion is that one is free to worship as they see fit. One's worship is that person's business; I think that our nation's business affects all, including those without any religious beliefs. Does not our Constitution call for our government to act on behalf of our entire nation regardless of belief?

Allow me to cite an example of political conduct I find deplorable. Many refer to this conduct as negative campaigning. I refer to it as disgraceful campaigning. President Obama was cast in an advertisement as a celebrity using as a backdrop two white female entertainers. These women were not elected by their communities to represent them because of their outstanding services, and they do not have outstanding college educations, either.

What is bothersome to me is that, from my experiences, any time a black man is displayed with white women in the manner in which President Obama was displayed with these two women, it represents racism. The subliminal message says, "Look at his race. Here is a black man who does not know his place." In President Obama's case, it is said that he was being referred to as a celebrity. My question is, why was he not compared alongside images of Angelina Jolie and Halle Barry, or images of Nicole Kidman and Drew Barrymore—women who a majority of society perceives as outstanding contributors to the arts and society in general?

The two women with whom he was displayed are best known to society for their outrageous behavior. Again, it seems to me that this was degrading to the character of President Obama. If one person feels he or she can be a better president than the other, then that person should discuss the issues and emphasize one's own qualifications. President Obama gave an incredible speech on racism. It's my belief that he was hopeful that race would not become a major factor within this election process. Regrettably, race and gender were injected into the campaign.

As a child growing up, I was taught to study hard, get good grades, and apply myself. By doing so, I could achieve any goal I desired. As I analyzed my surroundings, I realized that the teaching had a fallacy. If you were black, your options were limited. As an adult, I have seen major improvements in racial relations. In fact, I believe our country has almost reached the stage whereby the ability of the individual is considered the most important criteria by a majority of our citizens.

Only in America could President Obama have been elected to represent a major political party much less become President. Anyone thinking otherwise needs to visit other progressive countries and study their political systems. As Americans, we can feel proud of this fact and not be afraid to let others know that we have a great country. We must also draw attention to issues that need improvement.

During the last election process, I was hoping our candidates running for elective office, would not travel down the path of attempting to defile ones character or demean one's ability. Again my optimism was misplaced. Once it became obvious that candidate Obama was a serious contender with the possibility of being elected president, little subliminal messages began to be spoken by some, suggesting he was not qualified for the job as prescribed by the United States Constitution. Others overtly attacked candidate Obama as not being patriotic enough; a few even questioned Mrs. Obama patriotism because of a remark she made. By that time I had already became an Obama convert. His campaign was discussing issues and not personal individual attacks, which was refreshing. They should not have been attacking the individual because; Senator McCain is an outstanding citizen who has done tremendous things for our country.

To Senator McCain's credit he tried to keep his campaign focused on issues however a few people whom is often referred to as the extreme right wing element of the Republican Party refused to follow Senator McCain's wishes.

Senator McCain points out the fact he has had the ability to cross party lines to get things accomplished within the Senate. This is commendable, is it not what we elect our representatives to do? Senator McCain spent eighteen years within the Senate before he decided he could better serve our nation as President. President Barack Obama went into the Senate and served for a couple of years before coming to the conclusion that America's business was not being accomplished in the most efficient and productive manner.

Therefore, he decided to run for the office of President, not because he knows everything or that he can correct all of our nation's problems. To me, President Obama possesses unique characteristics one of Americans greatest citizens and three of

Americans Outstanding Presidents possessed. Please allow me to share what I see was the uniqueness of those individuals, and their greatest asset in contributing to our nation.

First is President Abraham Lincoln. This was a man who had the ability to give dynamic speeches, such as his Lyceum Address in 1838 at the age of twenty-eight, his Temperance Address at the age of thirty-three, his House Divided Speech in Springfield, Illinois, on June 16, 1858, and his most dynamic speech in 1863, the Gettysburg Address. While this was a speech that every generation of Americans learned and deeply valued, if asked, most Americans would not be able to describe the occasion for which it was written Another great speech that has journeyed over time and generations was President John F. Kennedy's inaugural address, delivered on January 20, 1961. It was a speech that inspired a nation, one that reflected the conditions of our country at that time. Two of the most remembered sentences of that speech are: "And so, my fellow Americans: ask not what your country can do for you—ask what can you do for your country" and "My fellow citizens of the world: ask not what America will do for you, but what together we can do for the freedom of man." President Kennedy was forty-three years old when he delivered this message to our nation, and he was forty-six when he was assassinated. Not once have I heard that he was too young and inexperienced or that all he could do was deliver a good speech.

President Ronald Reagan has been called the Great Communicator. His speeches have been termed "inspiring" and "reinvigorating," and many have contributed his rhetorical skills to the greatness of his presidency. Many failed to recognize his vision of "A shining city upon a hill" for America.

My final comparison is of another young man who is in the annals of American history—Dr. Martin Luther King Jr. Dr. King was the youngest Nobel Peace Prize Laureate at the age of thirty-five in April 1963. Dr. King wrote one of the most profound letters ever written. This letter was written while he was in jail and is titled, "Letter from Birmingham Jail." Again on August 28, 1963, Dr. King delivered his "I have a dream" speech at the steps of the Lincoln Memorial in our nation's capital. This speech was considered one of the most inspiring speeches ever delivered.

Dr. King was considered by many to be one of America's and the world's greatest advocates for the oppressed. His oratorical and prophesying skills were unequal in his day. America, are we not all better off today because of those skills, his intelligence, and his dedication to improving the conditions of his time? I have often asked myself, where would we, the people of the United States—especially black Americans—be today had it not been for Dr. King's oratorical skills? To many, this man was considered a prophet of and for the people.

What President Obama's contributions to America will be is unknown. So far, they are positive. I find it extremely asinine when people say that, while he delivers a motivating and inspiring speech, nonetheless, he has no experience—as if to suggest that there is no substance to the man. How much experience does one need to be intelligent? How much experience does one need to critically think and analyze situations to make reasonable decisions? I ask these questions because I'm a great-grandfather, have plenty of experiences, and pray every day that my children and grandchildren will make better decisions than I have made. My dreams are that they will live in a better society than I have and that they will contribute more to society than I have.

When President Obama was confirmed by proclamation at the Democratic National Convention, tears came into my eyes. As I looked and contemplated what had taken place, I could not help but feel a sense of joy, happiness, and pride. My internal emotions are hard to explain. There was joy that millions of Americans had come together and said, "We can work together. Your color doesn't matter; it's what you bring to the table that matters." There was joy that it was that woman who had challenged him for the nomination who made the motion for his nomination to be accepted by proclamation.

What was more gratifying was that this woman was a senator and a former first lady of the United States. She is a lady who is respected by many, one who ran a very close second for the nomination herself, the first of her gender to accomplish such goals.

The things that ran through my mind are very difficult to explain. I ask you to try to understand a sixty-seven-year-old black man who grew up in a segregated society. This same man, having gone into combat for his country, obeyed its laws and pledged his allegiance to a country he love. This same man prayed one day that he would see his country accept him and his offspring as equals. Then, on August 27, 2008, this man saw a majority of one political party in his country demonstrate that it was ready to move past racism and come together to do what is best for our country.

President Obama election as our president, said to the world that many Americans are willing to correct our past mistakes and move forward. America, I have always been proud of us. I have despised some of our behavior and questioned how long it would take before every citizen could say, "I am accepted as an equal." I realize that we have some distance to go before all Americans will accept one another as equals, but we have moved closer to this goal since the years of my youth, and I am grateful to you, my fellow countrymen.

We are making progress; at times, it seems the progress is moving slowly. Maybe it appears this way to me because I am coming into the twilight years of my life. I have held onto a faith that the people of America are good, kindhearted, caring, and will eventually get it right. The selection of this intelligent, articulate man of vision to lead our nation speaks volumes about the character of our nation. There are other areas I sincerely feel we must focus our attention on. My paramount concerns are for our smallest citizens—our children.

Our Depressing Economic Situation Causes Me Great Concerns

America, we are a nation of tremendous wealth. We are a nation with an economy unequal to any within the world. Yet we have millions of people living in our country as if they are living in what many call third-world or undeveloped nations. When I say we are a nation with an economy that is unequal, this statement is true at the present. However, if we are to believe what many of our expert economists are telling us, this may no longer be true in the near future.

One does not need to be an expert economist to recognize that something has to be terribly wrong within our country. When one goes into our retail stores to purchase items, the majority of the items are made in every country other than the United States of America. When I am shopping in these stores and reading these labels, I often ask myself, how can the American citizen survive? It appears to me that the focus of many of America's industries is misdirected. Let me explain my rationale for the previous statement.

Many of the items I have purchased over the years that are now made in other countries were once manufactured in the United States of America. How long can we continue to import a majority of the items consumed by the American public without providing adequate employment to purchase these items? At some point, the importation of merchandise has to affect this nation's ability to gainfully employ its citizens. My thoughts may appear to be illogical, but I ask that you consider the following point.

I own a sugar cane farm and employ ten workers. There is a sugar cane farm in another state from which I can buy sugar cane for less than I can produce it on my farm. I purchase from the farm in the other state and terminate my ten employees. Of course, I make more profit, but what have I done to ten families? I have created some amount of unpleasantness, if not hardship. Now we multiply my farm by one hundred farms, and we are speaking of a thousand families affected within my state. Why should I and the other ninety-nine farms care? We are getting richer. Is it not the former employees' responsibility to find other employment?

Three years later, the farms in the other state begin to increase their prices. No problem—we raise our cost. How long can we raise our cost before we begin to place a burden on the citizens of our state? Remember, we terminated one thousand employees. The funds they were expending within our state have been exported to another state. This means that my state has fewer funds generated from taxes and the money spent by those one thousand employees. This other state is prospering from revenue generated from taxes as a result of hiring additional employees, and that benefits both their state and their people.

The above is a simple analogy of a situation, but one I think reflects the state of affairs within our country. Many of our large industries have moved their manufacturing plants out of our country and into foreign countries where the cost of production is far less than it is in our country. Not only have they moved their plants to other foreign countries, eliminating much-needed employment within our country, but they are charging us, the consumer, to ship these materials back into our country for consumption.

It seems to me that something is unbalanced with this scenario. We have every industry one can imagine within the United States, following the scenario outlined above. Many industries, such as steel, automobile, textile, electronic, and so on are exporting their firms and shipping their products back into the United States. Personally, I have no objection to them exporting their firms to other countries. My objection is they are allowed to ship their products back into the United States. They moved their factories into foreign countries and employed people in those countries; they should be required to sell their products within those countries.

It's not that America has a shortage of people for these firms to employ; it's that these corporations are greedy, in my opinion. When our businesses and factories move their firms to a foreign country, purchase that country's raw materials, and employ its citizens because the standards of living in those countries are subpar to that of the United States, these firms cannot avoid causing undesirable effects on the citizens of the United States.

My belief is that, eventually, the working citizens of our country will become adversely affected. One cannot continue to consume what one has no participation in producing. For example, the South family of four has good employment at Moon's Factory. The North family of four is unemployed; they worked at Moon's but were laid off because Moon's moved a part of its firm to another country. The North family has been placed into a position of not being able to purchase anything. The family is not participating in the production; therefore, they cannot participate in the consumption.

One firm or one family is not a serious concern, but as the situation of this one firm and one family continues to multiply, the consequences become alarming. At some point over my years, I heard a narrative that was something like "One's first loyalty must be to one's family." If one's first loyalty must be to one's family, is not that family's loyalty expected in return? Are we, the people of the United States, not one family? Do we not pledge an allegiance to the United States as one nation under God? Does this not imply that we are uniting as one for the good of our nation? Are not businesses within the United States a part of this one?

If one accepts the above hypothesis, then is it not unreasonable to expect our economic industries of the United States to place emphasis on employing citizens of the United States first? From my viewpoint, America is a prosperous nation, made so by the family members of this nation. Do not those family members who have the ability to manage and operate our economic industries also have a responsibility to those family members of less intellectual and creative ability? When the citizen family of the United States is unified, do we not achieve stupendous goals? America, I believe we must educate, train, and employ the citizens of the United States.

As I write this book, I'm seeing the devastation of many lives because of conduct such as described above. We are a Country of wealth, yet too many of our children are at risk. Often, we look at the child already homeless or the child infected with deviant behavior, as being the Youth-at-Risk. Many children unborn are already at risk. Their parents cannot receive proper prenatal care. Many of these parents are unemployed, or have employment that pays to little for them to get proper nutrition, much less prenatal care.

Millions of America's citizens are entrenched in situations over which they have no control. I often ask myself, are not economic industries American citizens? Many of these industries will answer no and say, "We are American corporations." I will agree with this argument, and my response would be that *American* is the optimal word here. Many citizens of this nation place their lives in danger for these industries to grow and produce for the American people.

These same citizens love helping the people of other nations; many do it gladly every day. I think many feel as I do that we, as common citizens of our nation, deserve better than we are receiving from many of our economic industries. Americans, we will not get anything better or different unless we are willing to demand that we Americans come first in employment, health, and security.

Many Americans will ask, how can one citizen demand these things? I think there are several ways. Let me share a few of my thoughts with you. We start by registering to vote and voting in every election. We organize community groups to discuss issues of importance to our community and form coalitions to lobby our elective officials on those priority issues. Working Americans should be particularly concerned with electing individuals favorable to workers' unions.

We must study our elected representatives' record for accomplishing our desires. Should his/her record prove unfavorable, we elect someone else. Over the years it appears to me, many of us continue to reelect, many of our representatives because of their seniority. Seniority, only matters when one is effective in administering ours concerns. America our elected officials are the representatives of the people, I often question why is it that the majority of our middle class is ignored until election time.

Let me discuss Labor Unions, another means by which I believe American workers can improve their working and overall economic conditions. Labor unions as we know them today did not exist prior to 1800. There were small guilds, joint associations of employers and crafts people. They pressed for professional standards and restriction on outside competitors. These interests typically benefited the employee and employer alike.

However, these small guilds and joint associations changed with the Industrial Revolution. The invention of new production technologies, mass-production techniques, and an influx of semiskilled and unskilled workers attracted by employment opportunities migrated from the rural to urban areas and created a need for change. This migration of workers created a situation where these new economic industries could take advantage of the workers by paying low wages and low benefits. Few rights existed for hourly wage earners; their gains were solely dependent on their employer. This seems similar to the situation we are in today.

The emergence of national labor unions can be attributed to the realization of many workers. Those large and more powerful labor organizations were necessary to balance the increasing power of the corporate form of ownership. Today, our economy is considered one of the world's global economies. This implies to me the need for labor organizations who can address the needs of this economy.

In states that have laws restricting workers' rights to form strong unions, the average pay for all workers is lower. The so-called right-to-work laws, which limit workers' rights to collective bargain contracts (including wages and benefits), are a bad deal for all workers. In 2001, the average pay in right-to-work states was 15 percent lower than in states where workers have the freedom to form strong unions.

Let's examine the benefits of labor unions versus non-unions as they exist today. Labor unions have had a substantial impact on the compensation and work lives of both unionized and nonunionized workers. According to the U.S. Department of Labor statistics, in the year 2000, union workers earned significantly higher wages than nonunion workers did. For example, the average union worker earned $750.00 per week compared to $617.00 for nonunion workers—a difference of $133.00 per week.

Union workers could also claim similar advantages in virtually every occupational category and/or job classification. In nearly every occupational category, union members earned more than nonunion workers. For example, comparing the occupations of administrative and clerical personnel, union members earned $613.00 per week, while nonunion members earned $490.00 per week, a difference of 20 percent. Let's look at a couple of other occupations. Service-protective union members earned $820.00 per week, while nonunion workers earned $519.00 per week, a difference of 36.7 percent. Farm, forestry, and fish union members earned $548.00 per week, while nonunion workers earned $357.00 per week, a difference of 34.8 percent.

As the above paragraph illustrates, there are tremendous differences in the wages regardless of occupation. There are also other differences. Let's look at benefits. The difference in benefits is far more significant. This same document cites that the total benefit cost for nonunion workers was $6.38 per hour, compared with $12.41 per hour for union workers, almost double the nonunion rate. When legally required benefits were excluded, union benefits were worth $9.46 per hour, more than double the $4.38 per hour value of nonunion benefits. Benefits represented 37.4 percent of total compensation for union workers, the highest portion ever recorded, compared with 27.6 percent for nonunion employees.

Health benefits for union workers cost an average of $3.41 per hour; more than double the $1.42 per hour cost for nonunion workers. The $3.41 hourly cost was up from $2.17 in 2000. Health care benefits represented 10.3 percent of total compensation for union workers, again, the highest share ever recorded. Real union wages remained roughly flat while health care costs continued to soar. Benefits in general and health benefits in particular represented an ever-larger part of total compensation.

Foster, A.C., (2003). Differences in Union and Nonunion Earnings in Blue-collar and Service Occupations.

Am I pro-union? Yes. Do I advocate unions for all occupations? No. However, I do advocate a decent wage for all working Americans. The workforce today is much different from the way it was at the turn of the century. For example figures taken from the same document as above states, between 1900 and 2005, the percentage of the workforce that was white collar grew from less than 18 percent to 62.6 percent. While manual workers comprised 41 percent of the workforce in 1950, by 2005, their proportion had shrunk to only 23.5 percent of the workforce. The workforce is also more equally comprised of men and women. In 2005, women accounted for almost 47 percent of the workforce, up from 29 percent in 1950. In 2005, women were the majority of professional and related workers (56.3 percent) and were the majority of office and administrative support workers (75 percent). Women were also the majority of those who worked in service occupations (57.3 percent).

The service sector was and will continue to be the dominant employment generator in the economy, adding 18.7 million jobs by 2014. Almost 60 percent of all new jobs created in the United States between 2004 and 2014 are expected to be in the service- and professional-related occupations. While employment in the service sector will increase" or "While employment in the service sector has increased by almost 17 percent, manufacturing is expected to decrease by over 5 percent between 2004 and 2014. The number of bachelor's degrees expected to be conferred in 2012 is 21 percent greater than in 2000, the number of master's degrees, 19 percent greater, first-professional, 20 percent greater and PhDs, 5 percent greater.

Foster, A.C., (2003). Differences in Union and Nonunion Earnings in Blue-collar and Service Occupations.

The changing market for employees requires labor organizational changes, and it does not matter whether they are called labor unions or whether they adopt another name. What matters is that labor organizations become advocates, rallying for American economic industries to employ American citizens at a livable wage before outsourcing the work or importing foreign citizens into this country for employment. I also think that labor organizations must become our biggest advocates for better training and education.

Unions have had a substantial impact on the compensation and work lives of both unionized and nonunionized workers. Unionized workers earn significantly more in wages than nonunion workers. Differences in benefits are far more significant, especially in health care and retirement benefits.

America, with today's technological inventions and the ability to transport consumer products globally, do not American workers need the ability to organize again to protect their interests? I strongly suggest electing officials who strongly support organized labor—not with words, but with action.

Our young people of tomorrow are at risk of losing meaningful employment to citizens of other nations. Again, without the means of participating in the production, how can one participate in the consumption? One needs the income from participation in the production to be able to participate in the consumption. When one cannot participate in the production, that person is left with no alternative other than to rely on others to supply his or her needs. We do this through our social programs, unemployment funds, and the criminal justice system. It seems to me that there has to be a better solution. Let's talk, America. We can find positive, workable solutions better than those we are employing at present.

We ask our young people to respect our mores of America. We depend on our young people to defend our country against all enemies, foreign and domestic. Should we not have an expectation that our nation will protect our jobs? I agree with free trade, but should free trade cost American jobs? Maybe I don't understand the meaning of free trade. Should we not expect other nations to purchase our products because they are the best-quality products in the world? Purchasing and importing products—many of which are substandard—from other countries only because they can be procured less expensively is anti-American.

We often hear our political representatives calling on the citizens of America to place America first. When we export jobs or import citizens of other countries to America to fill highly technical jobs, are these political leaders and our industries placing Americans first? Are not the citizens of America what make America? We have heard and read several statements suggesting that American firms have to import qualified personnel from other nations to fill many of our technical jobs because America doesn't have enough qualified personnel.

If comments like the above are correct, then we, the leaders of our nation and the leaders of our industrial complexes, have failed the American citizens. Do we not have an obligation to train and educate Americans? Don't we have a responsibility to care for Americans first? I cannot speak for many Americans who have gladly given their lives for the defense of our country and the ideas our country expresses, but I can speak for one who has gone into combat and spent twenty-two years in the armed forces of our country, willing to sacrifice my life for the betterment of my family and countrymen. I feel great when America accomplishes great feats. I am one of those who gets a lump in my throat when our national anthem is played or when our national symbol is displayed.

Not only do I get emotional when the national anthem is played and our flag is displayed, but I also get mad as hell when another country speaks ill of or displays negative actions toward our country. I am not the only one who feels this way; I know and have known many outstanding American citizens who share these emotions. I knew several who gave the ultimate—their lives. I know others that are disabled for life; one of these is my closest friend. We must speak out and raise our voices. It matters.

Several major events occurred in 2008—events which will greatly affect each of us within the United States that I must comment on. The first one is Hurricane Ike; Hurricane Ike devastated much of Texas and the Gulf Coast of the United States. Looking at the devastation, one could not help but feel great empathy for those affected by the hurricane. Feeling empathy for those affected does not help alleviate their suffering. Many of these people have lost their entire lives' possessions.

Starting over is going to be very difficult for many of them. Some of these people have lost their jobs as well as their homes and personal possessions. My heart cries out to them and especially to those with small children. This hurricane was a natural disaster, an event which was humanly impossible to avoid. Yet those of us that were not affected directly cannot help being affected emotionally. Think of the children made homeless, those who have been forced from going to school to relying on the kindness of others for food and shelter. My hope is that each of us assisted those affected in whatever way we possibly could have. It is this next series of events that's bothersome—in fact, appalling—to me.

These events are the failure of many of our largest economic institutions. Their failure to survive does not bother me as much as the actions of our federal government in bailing them out of trouble did. The small mom-and-pop establishments of our country that run into financial difficulty must rely upon themselves to find the capital to continue operating or close shop. Of course, I well understand the adverse effects on the citizens of the United States had our government not come to their rescue. My questions and concerns are about our government allowing these institutions to deteriorate to that point.

Many will argue that the government had no choice other than to bail them out of their difficulties. While I am not intelligent enough nor have I any experiences in running global financial institutions, I have a good deal of experience in managing my personal finances. I know that I cannot continue to spend more money than I earn. A few months of conduct of this nature would have me filing for bankruptcy. Right or wrong, many of our government officials have decided for the good of the citizens of the United States that taking action to bail these institutions out of their financial difficulty was the correct thing to do.

There are many other aspects to this calamity that bother me with regard to our political leaders. Many of these people have been in public office for years. They have seen our economic institutions enriching themselves of the labors of the American workers. They have seen the wages of American workers deteriorating. They have seen both adults of households employed, and yet those adults still cannot afford to send their children to college. Yet Congress found it impossible to establish a minimum wage law at a rate that would ensure that every American family willing to work could live above the poverty level.

Many of our elected officials are quick to say that bailing out these financial institutions was not bailing out Wall Street, but was rather assisting Main Street and the small business establishments. Many, including myself, question the accuracy of their statements. Where was their concern for the small business establishments and Main Street when our large corporate businesses were moving into communities? These large organizations forced several small businesses out of business, eliminating the entire employment system of many families.

Many of these same officials were quick to say that these activities represent capitalism. They believed regulations and oversight were interference, that stronger and best-managed corporations were best for America. While this argument has validity, there is another side to the argument. The other side is that, if one allows anything to grow without controls, eventually it will become uncontrollable. One can argue that America, or at least our government officials, allowed many of our huge industrial and financial organizations to grow beyond control.

One cannot help but question how a country—or the government of such a country—could allow and support major industries within its borders to move into a foreign country and then allow those industries to import their products back into their country. And how can many of our elected officials complain that the social programs assisting the poor are unaffordable, and yet they ask the poor and middle class to contribute $700 billion to bail out companies that pay their chief executives millions in salary per year?

As stated earlier, I am against honest, hardworking Americans supporting individuals and the dependents of individuals who continuously commit criminal acts. I believe in charity. Those who lost everything in the two major hurricanes mentioned and those who have suffered devastating natural disasters of any sort deserve our support. Those industries that act against the interest of our people and nation don't deserve our assistance. Again, I am lacking in ability and knowledge concerning management of our nation's affairs. However, I do have opinions, and every American citizen has opinions. Let us express them. Maybe more of us think alike than do our government officials.

We must always remember that our government represents the people, and their authority is derived from the people. Within the past year, millions of Americans have lost their homes and jobs. What happens to these people and their families? Many of these families have become homeless. How do those parents feed or clothe their kids? More importantly, how does one explain to a child that the family is without the basic necessities to live because of greed and a lack of business and government officials' integrity?

My hope is that these same government officials will find some means of assisting our homeless, as well as those that have no health care, those that are jobless, and our mentally and physically disabled veterans. As stated throughout my writing, I love the United States and support our government. I will not always approve of decisions made, but I will support those decisions when they are debated and conclusions are determined by knowledgeable personnel.

It appears from what little information has been made available to the public—or that I am aware of—that the financial ruins of those institutions that have recently failed were due to greed and deliberate deception against many Americans—those that could least afford being taken advantage of. The destruction of those financial institutions came about because of individual and corporate greed. Actions like those attributed to the mortgage industry seem to be actions of a possibly criminal nature.

What baffles me is that the individuals that were responsible for monitoring the activities of our financial institutions to ensure that they operated in the best interest of the people of the United States failed their obligation. My understanding of the situation is that the same individuals responsible for the failures are the ones asking the American citizens to place their trust in them to manage the cleanup. It is said that they are the ones with the expertise to rectify the conditions. This supposition I seriously question.

For several days, we were told that our Congress debated the idea of whether to cast a line out to those sinking institutions, finally deciding that it had no other choice. Not supporting the bailout would have been too great of a cost for the citizens to bear. We were told that all credit transactions would come to a halt. What has been the cost to those who loss homes, jobs, and dignity? One group of our elected representatives was in favor of allowing these institutions to fail. The other group was opposed for the welfare of their constituents.

Either way, it seems to me that all of our national elected officials failed the majority of Americans. Were they not elected to serve the best interest of the American people? How many hardworking Americans lost homes to these mortgage institutions? The Americans who lost their homes were and are still taxpaying citizens whose funds had already been used to prop up two major mortgage institutions. It has been reported that the chief executive officers were entitled to between $9 and $15 million in compensation for their failures. Some call it a "golden parachute."

For simplicity's sake, let's use the $15 million figure. This figure amounts to $300,000.00 per year for fifty years. America, I can live comfortable with much less than that amount per year. The figure quoted does not include yearly salary. I have no problem with the amount they are being compensated. My problem is that we have a government elected to represent their people that failed their people.

Not only did several fail in their fiduciary duties, these same officials are asking the public to return them to their offices. Had the two major financial institutions been the only ones to fail, one could be somewhat forgiving of our government for falling asleep on its shift. However, when one hears the president of the United States and all major leaders of each political party plead with the American people to help finance an entire financial system to avoid devastating consequences to the nation, it is time for major changes.

How do we, the public, make major changes? May I suggest that we study the makeup of our government committees and their responsibilities? I also suggest that we fail to reelect the members of those committees who were responsible for oversight and failed their responsibilities. In fact, I suggest that we seriously evaluate all members of Congress for their effectiveness. Are they as effective for their average constituents as they are for the special interest groups? We need to vote those that fail our expectations out of office.

This will require something that we the citizens of America have failed to do. We have failed to become involved. When one examines our voting statistics as a nation, we come up deficient. Our largest voter turnouts are in presidential election years, and we have not exceeded over 60 percent of our population voting since 1968. In years in which other national, nonpresidential elections are held, the percentage has only exceeded 40 percent three times in forty-six years—45.4 in 1962, 45.4 in 1966, and 43.6 in 1970. Data taken from the same source suggests that approximately 66 percent of the voting-age population was registered to vote. U.S. Census Bureau, (2007) Statistical Abstract.

We must change our habits if we expect our elected officials to change theirs. Events within the last few months of my writing this book have created reason for much greater concern for our middle-class and poor populations.

When I started this book, I had no idea what I would say. I only knew that seeing those people lying around the New Orleans superdome and convention center without anyone assisting them with the basic necessities to survive hurt me. I started with sharing small portions of my life experiences in America as I have experienced them with you. I have shared my number one heartache, which is the number of our young children who have been neglected by parents and society. I have pleaded, asking us to work together and eliminate many of the conditions that exist for these children.

Throughout this writing, I have expressed my opinions on various topics. I do not profess to have the answers, and I do not say that my opinions offer sufficient solutions. I only request that we, the people of America, discuss the issues. By discussing them in an intelligent manner, we will find the correct solutions. I also requested that our nation not act as if we are not a nation with much racism displayed by many. When one avoids a fact, he or she perpetuates ignorance among those whom display this conduct.

Earlier in this writing, I mentioned a group of men with whom I had the privilege and distinct honor of serving as a member of their fraternity. I spoke of their contributions to society. As I stated earlier, these men have been in the trenches of our economically depressed communities and assisting those in despair. Many of these men are from economically depressed communities themselves and have very little to offer other than their time and encouragement to the young people of these communities. I love and respect these men. Many of them display the same racist attitude that much of society displays. Most of them like the majority of our nation are coming to terms and realizing that when we are united together, we accomplish much more.

Men I know who belong to this fraternity have been some of America's most outstanding and productive citizens. This organization also endures many of the same challenges of other organizations with which I have been allowed the privilege of membership. They have not been as selective as they should have been in accepting membership into them. The purpose of this organization from its beginning has been humanitarian in nature. Over centuries, it has espoused good government, good education for the citizens of their nations, and freedom to worship as one chooses.

Having been associated with this organization for forty plus years and having served as one of its state's presidents, as well as my association with other state presidents, I came to the conclusion that there is no organization equal in positive contributions to our nation. My friends, I honor your service to our country as much as I honor our military personnel's service to our country. My only request is that we return to our creed of only accepting men of like qualities and not the glory seekers.

In this writing, I have spoken on my limited experiences and what I have learned from them. I have spoken of my love of this nation. You have read the narrative of my beginning in America. I don't know how my ending will be, but I am proud of the United States of America. I started out in a segregated society and was educated in schools that were subpar, and yet

I have received a good education. I was born into poverty, and yet today I live a fairly comfortable life of retirement in the paradise of Hawaii. I have grandchildren going to outstanding public and private educational institutions.

My children are employed and are trying to live the American dream. My spouse and I are among the fortunate—we have good medical care. This journey for me has not always been pleasant. It has required sacrifices and heartaches, but please believe me—we are not complaining. I chose the military to assist me in my journey to live a successful life, and it has been good. One of my sons chose the military to start; he did not stay on active duty until he retired. He used it as a beginning—getting out, joining the reserves, going to college, getting a degree, and becoming a police investigator working for the State of Alaska.

None of my other children became members of the military, but all have successful occupations and are trying to improve life for their children. This is the American dream. I am thankful that my family is able to enjoy the benefits while contributing back. I can trace my family's history in America back to 1821; we started as slaves and farmers. My father broke the farmer tradition, and his son and grandchildren have improved their living standards substantially compared to his own and those of our ancestors. Where else other than American can one say they could have made such progress over such a short period of time?

Fathers, I have spoken to and pleaded with you on several occasions in this writing. My message to you is that we, the fathers of the United States, from the most destitute to the wealthiest, can change the lives of many of our youth at risk. We can only change these lives by being committed to changing them. We must be there for our children regardless of our economic conditions. We are role models whether we choose to be or not, and our society reflects the example we demonstrate.

America, we are a great nation, but we will never be the nation we can be without lifting all of our people. We must place our top priority on our children. They are our future, and their education and training is our security. We must look within, train within, produce within, educate within, and allow the reflections of our actions toward one another to radiate to other nations. Most important of all is that, as Americans, we must speak out and raise our voices. It matters!

As I come to the close of this book, our future appears to have a few difficulties ahead. Remember—our history tells us that when we come together, there is no challenge we cannot overcome. Together we must reclaim the attributes that made this nation the inspiration of people all over the world.

Love, Peace and happiness!

BIBLIOGRAPHY

Foster, Ann C. (2003). Differences in Union and Nonunion earnings in blue-collar and Service Occupations, Bureau of Labor Statistics. Retrieved from http:// www.bls.gov/opub/cwc/cm20030623ar01p1.htm October 2007

Kozol, Jonathan (1992). Savage Inequalities, children in America's school. Harper Perennial

Stephens, James J. (2001) state Prison expenditures Bureau of Justice Statistics special report. Retrieved from hhtp:// www.ojp.usdoj.gov/bjs/pubalp2.htm#spe

U.S. census Bureau (2007). Statistical abstract, the national data book. Retrieved from http://www.cencus.gov/compedia//statab/2007 elections html

Hawaii Department of Public Safety (2007). Annual report to the 2008 legislature, report No 2, exhibit B

Index